The First Nova Scotian

Mark Finnan

Formac Publishing Company Limited

Formac Publishing Company Limited acknowledges the Department of Canadian Heritage and the Nova Scotia Department of Education and Culture in the development of writing and publishing in Canada. We acknowledge the Canada Council for the Arts for its support of our publishing program.

Canadian Cataloguing in Publication Data

Finnian, Mark, 1944-

    The first Nova Scotian

    ISBN 0-88780-410-1 (pbk.)

1. Stirling, William Alexander, Earl of 1567?-1640. 2. Annapolis Royal (N.S.) — History. 3. Nova Scotia — Colonization. 4. Nova Scotia — History To 1784.*

FC2321.1A43F56 1997   971.6' 01   C97-950189-x

F1038.A43F56 1997

Photo Credits
Canadian Heritage Atlantic Region, Birgitta Wallace Ferguson collection - p. 9; 80; 90; 144; 145; 146; 148; 149; Finnan, Mark - p. 7; 10; 89; 99; 129; 137; 138; Historic Scotland - cover; p. 26; 43; 57; 111; Keddy, Bruce - p. 157; Lorimer, J.L. - p. 11; McCalla, Peggy - p. xii; National Archives - p. 85; Public Archives of Nova Scotia - p. ix; 108; Thibert, Hélène - p. 79; back cover

Formac Publishing Company Limited
5502 Atlantic Street
Halifax, Nova Scotia
B3H 1G4

Contents

For
Hélène and Elizabeth

who believe that
nothing is a more fitting tribute to our
past than to give it the future it deserves

Acknowledgements

The writing of any book, although a solitary experience, is never the work of the writer alone. I owe thanks to a number of people who helped make this one possible.

These include Dawn Campbell of the Municipality of Annapolis County and Peggy Armstrong of Granville Beach. During my stay in the Annapolis Royal area, I appreciated the time spent with Dorothy Thorne and Jim How of the Historical Association of Annapolis Royal. The Rev. Jim MacIntosh helped me trace the history of Freemasonry in Annapolis Royal, and John Kirby of Annapolis County's Historic Restoration Society took the trouble to show me through the building where the first official Lodge met. Dr. Barry Moody of the Department of History at Acadia University shared his extensive knowledge with me, and Professor Margaret Conrad, also of Acadia, explained to me the workings of the Historic Sites and Monuments Board of Canada. In my research through its Special Collections section, I was readily assisted by the staff at Acadia University's library. I thank Lillian Stewart and Theresa Bunbury for permission to carry out research at historic Fort Anne. My search through maps and manuscripts there was made all the easier and more enjoyable by Nora Saulnier. John McPhee of *The Spectator* in Annapolis Royal obliged with file material. Paula Barrett's log home at Parker's Cove, overlooking the Bay of Fundy, was a pleasure to both live and work in.

Carman Caroll and the staff of the Public Archives of Nova Scotia in Halifax readily answered queries and provided the appropriate research material. Scott Robson, Curator of Special Collections at the Nova Scotia Museum of Natural History, took the time to show me a badge of the Order of the Baronets of Nova Scotia. My brief discussion with Professor John Reid of Saint Mary's University in Halifax was also informative.

Birgitta Wallace Ferguson, Staff Archaeologist at the Halifax office of Parks Canada, Canadian Heritage, willingly shared both her discoveries at Fort Anne and her considerable expertise with me, and she made the writing of this book more interesting and pertinent.

Historian Brenda Dunn of the same office was helpful in providing background information about the "Scots Fort," and I appreciated having access to the conclusions of artifact expert Denise Hensen.

Bruce Rickett and Wayne Kerr of Canadian Heritage in Halifax were informative on Fort Anne matters, past and present. Dr. Marie Elwood of Indian Point provided me with several helpful early research suggestions. Diana Jarvis Reid and Carol Goddard of the Canadian High Commission in London provided contacts, and Professor Naomi Griffiths of Ottawa's Carleton University effectively clarified some points about her discovery of Richard Guthry's letter.

I am grateful to the Cultural Affairs Division of the Nova Scotia Ministry of Education and Culture for providing financial assistance toward the cost of travel to England and Scotland. My stay in England was made all the more fruitful and pleasant by Elizabeth Green of Claygate, Surrey.

The staff at the British Public Records Offices in Kew and Chancery Lane helped me make efficient use of my research time, as did their Edinburgh counterparts at the Scottish Record Office and the National Library of Scotland. The text of the Guthry letter is included by permission of the Keeper of the Records of Scotland. I wish to thank Jane Ferguson, Joseph White, and Dr. Richard Fawcett of Historic Scotland in Edinburgh, who promptly provided material about Sir William Alexander's birthplace in Menstrie and his Stirling manor house. Similar service was readily extended by Indira Mann of the National Trust for Scotland in Edinburgh. My research into Alexander's place in Scottish history was enlivened by the perspective of the knowledgeable Aonghus MacKenzie. Moira Mackay of Glasgow University and Veronica Steele of the National Monuments Record of Scotland, Architecture Section, Edinburgh, were prompt in replying to my queries, as was Susan Kerr of the Scottish National Portrait Gallery. Carole G. Seguin of the National Archives of Canada in Ottawa provided insightful answers to my queries.

For background information about the stone cairn honouring Sir William in Halifax, I am grateful to Donald MacLean. Staff at the Annapolis Royal, Bridgewater, and the Lunenburg Public Libraries were always helpful. Peta Mudie of Halifax provided technical assistance, and the Glens of Upper LaHave and the Adams of Chester shared maps and memories.

From the outset of this project, I was wholeheartedly assisted in many ways by Hélène Thibert. Finally, I have appreciated the excellent work of editor Scott Milsom and the interest of Jim Lorimer, Carolyn MacGregor, and the staff of Formac Publishing.

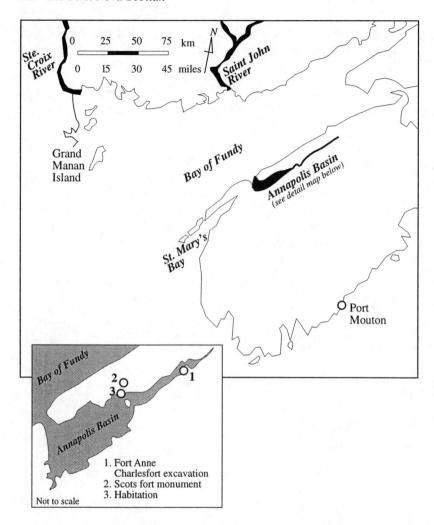

1. Fort Anne
   Charlesfort excavation
2. Scots fort monument
3. Habitation

Not to scale

Introduction

For over 360 years the precise location of the first English-speaking settlement in Nova Scotia, and on the mainland of Canada, remained unknown. The fact that there was no available written account describing the nature of the settlement and the day-to-day lives of its inhabitants only enhanced the aura of mystery. Nova Scotian historians have given scant attention to the man responsible for this settlement, first planned just after the Pilgrims arrived in Massachusetts, in spite of the fact that the Scottish-born poet, playwright, and statesman Sir William Alexander, a contemporary of Sir Walter Raleigh, William Shakespeare, and Sir Francis Bacon and confidant of two Stewart kings, also gave the province its name, flag, coat of arms, and its own chivalric order.

Now, thanks to the accidental discovery of a 368-year-old letter

The Armorial Achievement of Nova Scotia, granted by King Charles I in 1625

in the book-lined confines of the Scottish Record Office in Edinburgh and the coincidental unearthing of archaeological evidence long buried in southwestern Nova Scotia, we finally have some factual knowledge about this historic settlement. The newly discovered written material provides us with a description of the settlers' heroic voyage from England and their arrival on the shores of the Annapolis Basin in 1629. As well as pinpointing the settlement's exact location, its contents give us some sense of the early days of the settlement itself, and include personal observations about the appearance and lifestyle of the native Mi'kmaq, who befriended and traded with the settlers.

The existence of this settlement, governed by Sir William's eldest son and christened Charlesfort in honour of King Charles I, and its subsequent surrender to the French had repercussions that rippled out beyond the shores of Nova Scotia and continued to affect events into the middle of the next century. It can be argued that because Charlesfort gave England its first official foothold in Nova Scotia and was part of the first territory to be negotiated between, and later fought over by, the French and English in Canada, it has played a pivotal role in affecting the course of our country's history to this very day.

Yet few Canadians are even aware that the Annapolis Basin cradled the first attempts at mainland settlement in Canada. Here, the first French, Scottish, and English settlers built homes, planted crops, and raised children. Those who survived these early years in unexplored terrain did so in part because they were welcomed and helped by a friendly native population.

The predominantly peaceful Mi'kmaq camped upriver, fishing and hunting along the shores of the Basin. Here, for a few brief years at least, romantic legend, native lifestyle, and the dream of peaceful settlement in a land of plenty seemed to harmoniously converge, giving credibility to the notion raised by the early trans-Atlantic explorer, Giovanni da Verrazano, who compared the eastern seaboard of the "new world" to the mythological, pastoral kingdom of Arcadia. Such a notion lay behind both Thomas More's classic *Utopia* and Francis Bacon's *New Atlantis*, and it fired the imagination of some early adventurers and explorers. There are echoes of this in *An Encouragement to Colonies*, written by Sir William Alexander in 1624.

The immediate approval and extended support two British monarchs showed to his proposal to establish a New Scotland on the northeast coastline of North America had triumphant and tragic consequences for Alexander himself, who early in his life was infused with the creative spirit and literary ideals of the Renaissance. While giving unquestioned loyalty to the kings he served, his allegiances, aspirations, and accomplishments were not always understood or appreciated in his own country, as is evident in the comment of a fellow Scot who referred to him, perhaps with some degree of envy, as a man "born a poet who sought to be a king."

Like Shakespeare, as a playwright Alexander dared to advise, and even admonish, monarchs with his philosophical pen. As a poet, he drew on both Biblical and classical themes. His epic poem *Doomsday*, drawn from the Book of Revelation, ends with a descriptive vision of a New Jerusalem, and he completed Sir Philip Sidney's prose masterpiece *Arcadia*, which chronicled the triumph of enduring love in a pastoral utopia. Like James I, his legacy is that of unifier and peacemaker. To the land where he hoped his New Jerusalem would arise, he gave much of his time, energy, resources, and the name by which it is known to this day.

Much mystery still surrounds the history of Nova Scotia during the years of Sir William Alexander's association with it. According to carbon dating of materials found on Oak Island in Mahone Bay, the mysterious underground shafts there were likely being worked during this period. As I have already written in *Oak Island Secrets*, Alexander's access to Nova Scotia, and his close connections at court and to the Masonic Order (in which the monarchy was also involved) made him an ideal candidate to effectively carry out a highly secretive operation here that remains a mystery to this day.

Stone foundations and artifacts found on a property in the hillside village of New Ross in central Nova Scotia have not yet been investigated by any detailed archaeological dig or carbon dating. But Joan Harris, their discoverer and the property's former owner, believes that a structure resembling an early seventeenth-century English manor house once stood in her back garden. If her theory that it was built with the secret sanction of King Charles I is correct, then it also likely in some way involved Sir William Alexander.

I hope that by providing a reappraisal of the life and times of Sir William Alexander and uncovering some of the mystery surrounding Charlesfort, I can contribute to a more comprehensive and deeper knowledge of Nova Scotia's remarkable early history, a knowledge that can be enriching and inspiring to us both now and in the future.

Latter Day Pioneers

In the summer of 1975 I emigrated from Ireland to Canada with my wife, Deirdre, and three very young children. Having written several articles about our four–year experience of homesteading in rural Ireland, I had been invited to help set up a small, agrarian-based, cooperative community in Ontario.

As we stepped onto the plane at Dublin airport, after bidding our goodbyes to families and friends and a bitter-sweet farewell to the land of our birth, I had the sense that we were like a latter-day pioneer family setting out, as had so many before us, on a trans-Atlantic crossing to a more promising life on a new continent. Little did I think then that this journey would one day lead me to research into the life of a visionary, Renaissance man and to explore the site of his Nova Scotia settlement, both of which played a brief but pivotal part in the province's, and the country's, colourful and dramatic past.

Some four years earlier, following the birth of our son, Deirdre and I had left the increasingly crowded streets, competitive atmosphere, and polluted climate of London for what we hoped would be a less harried and healthier lifestyle on a two-and-a-half acre holding in Ireland. This move to the quiet Irish countryside, just south of the historic town of Wexford, with its unique challenges and demands, proved more rewarding in many ways than the life I had known in London as a struggling actor and writer.

I continued to write, of course, about our day-to-day, and season-to-season, activities. I learned and wrote about the art of composting and the benefits of companion planting, and shared the joys and sorrows of looking after a menagerie of hens, ducks, wandering goats, and a largely immobile donkey. We managed to convert a nearby disused store into a lively folk theatre, where the interactions between our real-life experiences and those on stage often created their own unique humor and drama. I was seldom short of subject material.

My writing was motivated by more than the prospect of having articles published and receiving the occasional cheque in the mail. Our desire to adapt to a healthier life and have our children spend their early years close to nature had unintentionally immersed us in the emerging, if unorganized, back-to-the-land movement in Ireland. I sent out my articles in the hope that others thinking or planning along similar lines might find some useful advice, inspiration, or support in them.

During our last year in Ireland one of my articles was published in a North American magazine and, shortly afterwards, I received a letter from a Canadian environmentalist outlining his interest in developing a rural-based, intentional community near Barrie, Ontario. A job offer was forthcoming and since it seemed to provide several advantages over our existing situation, it didn't take us long to make up our minds. So it was as a somewhat prepared and excited twentieth-century version of a new-world settler that I found myself and my family, on that August day in 1975, taking off on a plane to Canada.

Looking down at the wide expanse of the Atlantic, I realized we were following a route taken by millions of earlier adventurers and emigrants dating back through several centuries. Explorers, colonizers, merchants, and missionaries, men and women of every rank, race, and religion, crown princes and the impoverished, had crossed that vast sea before us. Most had set out hoping their journey would result in an improvement on the lives they were leaving behind. Some sought to escape religious oppression or political tyranny and hoped to find freedom on a far-away shore. Many had been driven by hardship and hunger into making a rough voyage across a vast ocean to an unknown land.

As I looked at my wife and children seated beside me, it occurred to me that timeless threads of thought and feeling linked us to those earlier adventurers and emigrants. Fortunately for us, our crossing was far more comfortable than many of theirs had been, and we were to face far fewer material challenges and hardships on our arrival in our newly adopted country. Yet, regardless of differences between us in time and circumstance, we shared some of the same outlook and were moved by some of the same mixed emotions that many of them must have felt — a sense of loss at parting from people and places long known and loved, and the sheer excitement of embarking on a new and, we hoped, rewarding adventure.

My first two years in Canada were preoccupied with meeting the challenge of creating a new life for myself and my family, and there was little time for writing. Most of my energy and time were taken up with helping to design, build, and manage a holistic lifestyle research-and-development centre in southern Ontario. A crew of four of us built a large, multi-purpose log chalet on a fifteen-acre site adjacent to a preserved wooded area. Hundreds of additional trees were planted on open ground, and an experimental windmill was designed, built, and put into operation. Extensive organic gardens were laid out and a solar greenhouse added to the main building. In-house and outreach programs were developed and contacts were made with many similar organizations and projects in Canada and the United States. Once up and running, we initiated and participated in conferences, workshops, and community events. It was a busy, demanding, and exciting time.

By the early 1980s, I had become part of an extensive network of individuals, groups, and organizations that were exploring new lifestyles and developing program that dealt with matters ranging from personal growth and alternatives in education to more environmentally appropriate habitat and sustainable development. Since many of our activities had political, social, cultural, and spiritual implications, there was a shared sense that our collective endeavours would one day bring about large-scale and constructive change.

Occasionally, it occurred to me that our own evolving project and the quiet but widespread movement of which we had become a part were, in some respects, modern-day equivalents of earlier efforts to forge new beginnings in the new world of seventeenth-century North America. But, beyond a few general ideas concerning the early history of the country, I knew practically nothing about the background to, or the location of, the first European settlements in Canada.

By the mid-1980s, I was working as a news director and broadcast journalist and so began to learn more about various aspects of Canadian history and geography. Covering municipal, provincial, and national political events, I acquired a working knowledge of the country's political past and, in the process became familiar with the opposing political and religious loyalties of Canada's first European settlers, the French and English, and the litany of their military machinations. I also became acquainted with the honour roll of trans-Atlantic adventurers who first sailed to these shores and the explorers who first ventured into our interior.

This on-the-job crash course in Canadian history prepared me to some degree for the more precisely focussed, in-depth historical research I embarked on after arriving in Nova Scotia in 1992 to work on a film script. While living near Mahone Bay on the province's south shore I wrote a book about the famous and ongoing Oak Island mystery, considered by many to be the longest, costliest, and most hazardous treasure hunt in history. During research for *Oak Island Secrets*, I learned that carbon dating of materials found on and beneath the island indicated that work had been carried out there sometime between the mid-sixteenth and late-seventeenth centuries. Full of international turmoil and colourful characters, it was a fascinating period to research. Extending from the years when Spanish galleons were escorting countless tons of gold and silver across the Atlantic from Central and South America, it encompassed a time of widespread pirate and privateer activity on the high seas. It was also the era that saw the beginning of English and French incursion into North America and the establishment of the first known colonies by both powers in present-day Nova Scotia. That was how I first came across Scottish-born poet, playwright, and statesman Sir William Alexander, who in 1621 gave Nova Scotia its name, flag, and coat of arms and, in 1629, its first British settlement.

From what I was able to read about him in the sparse material available, he was a multi-talented Renaissance man with interests ranging from literature to mining and trans-Atlantic adventuring. His poetry and plays were philosophical in content and suggested a man influenced by the literary ideals and aspirations of the Elizabethans. He had enjoyed the support and friendship of both King James I and his son Charles I and been associated with some of the most powerful people at court. As Secretary of State for Scotland, he had been granted a royal charter that gave him almost regal powers over the vast area that would be known as Nova Scotia.

In view of all this, I began to wonder whether Alexander might have been in some way associated with the mysterious workings found on Oak Island and the treasure still believed to be buried there. Adding to my suspicions were the stone foundations of an old building found on a hillside in New Ross at the headwaters of the Gold River, not far inland from Oak Island. Their discoverer, who owned the property at the time, seemed convinced that an English manor house had existed on the site, and she suggested that it had been built while Alexander had access to and jurisdiction over Nova Scotia.

My research also made me aware of the esoteric activities of the Masonic Brotherhood, to which Alexander and his sons were connected. These discoveries raised the possibility that Sir William Alexander may have been at least indirectly involved in secretive activity in Nova Scotia. My conclusions about such a possibility were presented in *Oak Island Secrets*.

The fact that so little was known about the several trans-Atlantic voyages Alexander sponsored (and that no descriptive account seemed to exist of the settlement of Charlesfort, administered by his eldest son, also named William) left me anxious to learn more about the man and his mission. However, apart from a few biographical references, some short articles, and a single chapter in a history of Nova Scotia, I could find no detailed account of him in Canadian historical material. To my surprise, Charlesfort, known to have existed on the shores of the Annapolis Basin, does not even get a mention on Nova Scotia maps, past or present.

The little I had learned about Alexander convinced me that he had been a major literary figure of his day, that he had exerted extraordinary influence on Scottish affairs, and that he had made a very important contribution to the ongoing efforts to colonize North America. I learned that his life had ended tragically, largely because of his commitment to permanent settlement in Nova Scotia. But, apart from a plain stone cairn and accompanying plaque in a Halifax park, there seemed to be no public acknowledgement of the man. That someone of his accomplishments, interests, and talents could remain so neglected seemed regrettable. Here, I felt, was an extraordinary figure worth remembering, a heroic story from Nova Scotia's and Canada's past that deserved telling.

So, several times during the summer of 1995 I gave serious thought to continuing my research into the life and times of Sir William Alexander and to writing a book about him and his lost colony of Charlesfort. Finally, in an effort to help me make up my mind on the matter and curious to see the lie of the land in which this long-forgotten settlement was believed to have existed, I set out in September of 1995 on an exploratory trip across Nova Scotia to the Annapolis Valley and Bay of Fundy area of the province. Little did I expect that my brief stay there would be as interesting and rewarding as it was.

2

Settlers' Valley

The highway that runs northwest from Halifax to Windsor and Wolfville and then turns southwest through the Annapolis Valley retraces a route travelled by Mi'kmaq and Acadians prior to the founding of Halifax in 1749.

Following old Highway 1 past Bedford, I pass through pleasant, rolling countryside that still bears traces of the eighteenth-century English settlers who lived there. Descending from the village of Ardoise into the valley where the St. Croix and Avon Rivers converge, I enter the town of Windsor, built up around the site of an earlier Acadian settlement.

After meandering along the west bank of the estuary of the Avon River through the still active port of Hantsport to Horton Landing, near where some of the first New England Planters of 1760 came ashore, I cross the Gaspereau River to historic Grand Pré, now commemorated in story and stone as the emotional heartland of the dyke-building Acadians of the Minas Basin. Heading due west to the attractive town of Wolfville, I stop to visit Acadia University. Its library's collection of documents and publications about the province's early history convince me I need to return to spend some research time within its walls. Crossing the street, I drop into the newly opened Festival Theatre, where a production of Shakespeare's *The Tempest* has just been presented. Like many other small university towns, it has the look and feel of being creatively alive.

Heading southwest again, I drive along the old road through the red-earth croplands and fruit fields of Annapolis Valley, which presents itself to me, as it must have even more strikingly to its first settlers, as a pleasantly sculptured and highly bountiful natural sanctuary. It's easy to imagine the sheer joy and relief early settlers must have felt when they first gazed upon this inviting and verdant valley.

Passing almost parallel to the lie of the gently rising North Mountain, which runs some 150 kilometres between Blomidon and

Fort Anne, Annapolis Royal

Digby Gut, a narrow opening to the sea at the far end of the Annapolis Basin, I pass through a succession of valley towns. The countryside between them is dotted with numerous small white churches, old farmhouses, and remnants of once-sturdy barns, silent reminders of the strongly held religious convictions and strenuous labours of the valley's pioneer families. Driving slowly alongside the Annapolis River, I imagine the many native Mi'kmaq, trappers, and traders who must have paddled between its banks. Living as we do in a highway-landscaped jet age, we often forget how practically important were sea and river to people of earlier times. After passing through such appropriately named hamlets as Paradise and Belleisle, I arrive at the causeway that crosses the river to my destination, the town of Annapolis Royal.

Having parked my car in the grounds of Fort Anne, the historically recognized site of the town's first inhabitants, I take the time to read some of the available literature.

According to the terms of the 1632 Treaty of Saint-Germain, which ended yet another round of hostilities between England and France, Nova Scotia, having been claimed by the English in the 1621 charter issued to Sir William Alexander, was returned to France and reverted to the name of Acadie. It is widely believed that the Fort Anne site was first occupied around 1636 by about 60 French families, military personnel, and missionaries. Over the next 75 years, there was a succession of English and French occupations, and after the British took and retained this strategic site in 1710 it was given its present name of Annapolis Royal. Not surprisingly, by 1749, when the administration of the colony moved from here to the newly established city of Halifax, evidence of the earlier settlement here had been well buried under many feet of raised and extended earth-work defences.

While walking around the raised perimeter of the site, I stand at its southern tip, struck by the awesome view it offers. Light from the late afternoon sun sparkles like liquid diamonds on the water below and coats the surrounding landscape of river, marshlands, mud flats, and hillsides in an early autumnal glow. Standing here looking over terrain that must have appeared even more remarkable to the valley's first European arrivals, I try to imagine what the original settlement of artisans and peasant families might have been like. Remembering the challenges of my own early days in Canada, I imagine how much more difficult theirs must have been. I feel certain that some of them must have occasionally taken time out from their demanding daily chores and endless toil to enjoy this same spectacular view. Putting doubts and fears about their future aside, some must surely have uttered silent prayers of gratitude for the beauty and bounty of their new home.

Later, I visit the Fort's museum, where, much to my surprise, I discover that the dominant display in the museum, a recently completed tapestry illustrating important historical events and people

The first Masonic Lodge in Canada

connected with the area over the last 400 years, does not show Sir William Alexander or the Charlesfort settlement of 1629. Answers from one of the staff to my enquiries about this apparent gaff are decidedly confused, and I get the distinct impression that neither had been considered significant enough to merit representation. These omissions from the colourful, hand-stitched tapestry seem even more puzzling to me when I observe, among the collected accounts and paraphernalia of other periods elsewhere in the museum, a copy of the Nova Scotia charter issued to Alexander by King James I in 1621. I conclude that a lack of local knowledge about Alexander and Charlesfort probably resulted in their being omitted.

Leaving the confines of Fort Anne, I stroll down Saint George Street to view some of its restored and renovated buildings and absorb some of the historical atmosphere of this unique town. I pass the Sinclair Inn where a plaque states that Nova Scotia's first Masonic Lodge gathered in an upstairs room. Just a few doors down the street is John Adams' house, now a restaurant and antique shop, where the first colonial government met. Beyond the market square lie other old buildings in various stages of restoration or renovation. At the street's end I rest by what had been the encampment of a group of Mohawk warriors brought from New York by the British during the early days of Annapolis Royal to help combat the Mi'kmaq-French alliance. The sight of the far shore is pleasant to contemplate, with its appealing view of the eighteenth-century settlement of Granville Ferry and the North Mountain rising behind it. My eye follows its crest southwestward, where it dips and disappears to allow an opening to the sea. Below me, half-buried in mud by the water's edge, I see the seaweed-covered remains of a long abandoned stone-and-timber wharf. I wonder if any Charlesfort settlers rowed ashore at this spot to explore the arm of high ground on which the town now stands.

Failing to find Charlesfort located on any historical or contemporary maps, but remembering a reference that it had probably been in the vicinity of Port Royal National Historic Park, the site of a reconstructed 1605 French settlement known as the Habitation, I re-cross the causeway and head down the Granville Road in its direction.

With an hour to spare before the Habitation closes I stroll through the authentically recreated confines of an early seventeenth-century rural French manor. Sitting in the large main hall, with its huge open fireplace, long wooden dining table, ornamentally carved chairs, and pewter-lined dresser, I look out through the open doorway onto the central courtyard where French-speaking, costumed guides chat to visitors or go about their chores. Bird-song from the nearby trees and the scent of garden herbs add a realistic backdrop to a setting straight out of that robust and romantic age of French maritime exploration, the era of the remarkable man from Navarre, King Henri IV. This outward-looking king sought to assert French claims to part of the then little-explored North American continent and to acquire for France its untapped riches and resources. It was with his approval and support that a group of Frenchmen, headed by Sieur de Monts and including Samuel de Champlain, crossed the Atlantic and built the original Habitation in 1605.

Before leaving, I learn from one of the guides that a "Scots Fort" was believed to have existed around the 1630s across the road from Port Royal National Historic Park. At last, I've found the site of Sir William Alexander's settlement of Charlesfort, or so I think. Hurrying off to find nearby accommodation, I take note of a stone cairn and plaque in a nearby field. Later that evening, I return to walk the ground where, according to the information on the plaque placed there by the Historic Sites and Monuments Board, Charlesfort once stood and the first British inhabitants of the province to be known as Nova Scotia made their homes, toiled, and dreamed of a future better than the past they had left behind. That night, savouring a glass of wine by the open fireside in a nearby country inn and recalling my own experience of settling in Canada and adapting to the many

The area near the Port Royal Habitation, originally believed to be the site of the "Scots fort"

changes involved, I feel sympathetically connected to those first hardy and hopeful settlers who came to these parts almost four centuries ago.

The next morning, after an early and unexpected wake-up call from the inn's highly vocal rooster, I take a stroll, intending to photograph the "Scots Fort" site in the rising sunlight. After taking several close-ups of the plaque commemorating the arrival of the Alexander settlers, I walk about the slanted land on which it stands, trying to imagine the fort's overall size and configuration. The absence of any illustrated site plan makes this quite difficult and I leave somewhat saddened by the obvious lack of any defining diagrams or markers, especially compared to the extensive display material at the elaborately reconstructed Habitation not far away.

Later, I cross the road to browse through a small souvenir store and savour an early-morning coffee in the adjoining restaurant. Sitting at an outside table, I strike up a conversation with a couple who had stopped by for breakfast. In the ensuing exchange of pleasantries, I learn they had just dropped off their young son for one of those marathon hockey tournaments that periodically stir many Canadian parents reluctantly to life in the wee small hours. Learning that the purpose of my visit to the area is connected to a prospective book about Sir William Alexander, the dedicated hockey mom introduces herself as Dawn Campbell, Heritage Clerk for Annapolis County. She tells me that her work includes coordinating and disseminating

Monument and plaque at the site near Port Royal

Aerial views of the Annapolis Royal area showing the location of the "Scots fort" at the perimeter of Fort Anne

information about the many historic sites in the area. After readily providing me with the names of several important local contacts, academics, and history buffs, she tells me about an archaeological dig undertaken during the previous few summers at Fort Anne. I listen both amazed and delighted while she informs me that the dig has unearthed evidence suggesting that Alexander's seventeenth-century settlement of Charlesfort may have been elsewhere than at the designated site of the "Scots Fort." She also tells me that a seventeenth-century letter, written in Nova Scotia, has surfaced in

Scotland that gives an account of the 1629 voyage of the Charlesfort settlers and also indicates that the settlement was much further up-river from the Port Royal Habitation than previously believed.

Charged by my good fortune at having had this serendipitous and informative meeting with Dawn, I hurry back to Halifax to visit the local offices of Canadian Heritage on Water Street, where I meet archaeologist Birgitta Wallace Ferguson. After I explain the purpose of my visit, she kindly shows me the elaborately documented and extensively photographed details of her four-year archaeological dig and the discoveries it has revealed at Fort Anne.

A discussion with Canadian Heritage historian Brenda Dunn leads me to the History Department of Saint Mary's University in Halifax for a brief meeting with Professor John Reid. I learn from him that he and Naomi Griffiths of Carleton University in Ottawa have published a scholarly paper entitled "New Evidence on New Scotland" in *The William and Mary Quarterly*, an American academic journal. Drawing from the contents of a lengthy and detailed letter written by one of the Charlesfort settlers, accidentally discovered by Griffiths in the Public Record Office in Edinburgh a few years earlier, it convincingly makes the case that the settlers did not go ashore near the Habitation, but in the area recently excavated by Wallace Ferguson at Fort Anne. Reid also tells me that the letter's author, a man named Richard Guthry, has provided a detailed account of the settlement's early days.

As I talk with the various people involved, examine numerous diagrams and slides, and read the written reports, I have a growing realization that one of Nova Scotia's longest-standing historical mysteries is in the process of being solved.

3

Exploring The Past

All these discoveries convinced me that I should spend some time in the area of the Charlesfort settlers, but I needed first to view the Guthry letter and other related documents as part of my research into the life and times of Sir William Alexander and his efforts to establish New Scotland. I also hoped that a visit to England and Scotland, where Alexander had lived and worked, would give me a better sense of the circumstances of his life and a fuller appreciation of his work as a poet, playwright, and statesman.

In January 1996 I set off on a mid-winter research trip to England and Scotland, but before leaving, I learned that at least two other long-lost documents relating to Charlesfort had surfaced on the other side of the Atlantic. According to John Reid, a second letter had been found in the Scottish Record Office in Edinburgh, the contents of which were more general than those in the Guthry letter. From Dr. Marie Elwood, formerly of the Nova Scotia Museum of Natural History, I learned that a third document relating to the 1629 voyage of the Charlesfort settlers had surfaced in London. At a morning meeting at her Tantallon home, she explained that it contained information about the passengers on one of the vessels that carried Alexander's settlers to Nova Scotia. Although unable to recall all the details, she was sure that much like a ship's log, it listed the names of the people on board and also the captain's name and that of the ship itself. This was confirmed by Carman Caroll, Chief Archivist at the Public Archives of Nova Scotia in Halifax, who had also seen a copy of the document. The provincial Archives had unfortunately been unable to meet the exorbitant asking price of a London dealer who had acquired the document, and as far as I could gather, it had been returned to England. It was suggested I contact one Peter Winkworth in London, who had been contacted by the dealer and first brought the matter to Dr. Elwood's attention. Although it apparently included nothing of the actual arrival of the settlers, I thought the document significant because of the dearth of existing material about the voyage. I hoped to have the opportunity to see it and read its contents.

Arriving at London's Heathrow Airport, I was pleased to be met by my sister Elizabeth and to enjoy the comfort and convenience of her cottage home at Claygate in Surrey. After catching up on lost sleep, I was greatly relieved the next day to discover that I would not have to make the long daily trek into central London, as I had expected, because much of the material relating to Alexander's activity at court and the Nova Scotia charter were available at the British Public Record Office at Kew, not far from where I was staying. Housed in a spacious, ultra-modern building, its archives contain a treasure trove of material from the earliest days of England's involvement in the colonization of North America. Perhaps only those who have done similar work can really know the enormous degree of anticipation and sheer excitement I felt, as I opened my first file of nearly 400-year-old papers.

As I carefully turned over page after page, the names of individuals, places, and events long written into history books floated off the delicate paper. File after file contained centuries-old official correspondence from the reign of Elizabeth I through that of James I to the time of Charles I. Among the documentation dealing with England's trans-Atlantic adventures, I came across references to Sir Walter Raleigh and his Virginia colony at Roanoke, to the historic Jamestown settlement, and to Sir John Guy and his colony at Cuper's Cove in Newfoundland. Eventually, I found several references to Sir William Alexander and his Nova Scotia enterprise. During the next week or so, I spent long hours digging deeper into the files.

Part of my time in England was also spent within the book-lined walls of the Victorian Round Room in the Public Record Office in Chancery Lane, the first building in the world designed for and dedicated to archival work. Here, I discovered, among other documents relevant to Alexander's time at court, material concerning the King's Master of Works, a position occupied by Alexander's second son Anthony, who had been an architect. His appointment directly involved the Alexander family in Masonic politics of the day and intimated that the monarchy itself was both interested in and knowledgeable of Masonic matters.

While in London, I attempted to trace the document, in the nature of a ship's log, that I had been told about in Nova Scotia. Through the help of Elizabeth Richie at the Canadian High Commission, I eventually spoke with Peter Winkworth, the person first contacted by the dealer. A man obviously interested in Canadian historical matters, he readily agreed to act as go-between, but the mysterious dealer could not be traced and nothing materialized.

On my last day in London, as I left the Overseas Club off Piccadilly, where I had given a luncheon talk about Oak Island to keenly interested members of the Maple Leaf Club, I was beginning to wonder whether I had stumbled into yet another Nova Scotia historical mystery involving enigmatic characters and ever-elusive hard evidence. Then I remembered what I had seen in archaeologist Birgitta Wallace Ferguson's office back in Halifax, and that in Edinburgh I would have a chance to read a letter written from Nova Scotia by someone who had sailed with Sir William Alexander's son in 1629 as a member of the Charlesfort settlement.

My time at the Kew and Chancery Lane archives had been quite informative in providing me with details about the background to Alexander's plans to establish a New Scotland. The documentary evidence abundantly indicated that Alexander's proposal had received extraordinary support from both King James I and his son Charles I. The records also dealt with the confusing political circumstances that contributed to the demise of Charlesfort.

I hoped that my time at the Scottish Record Office and the National Library in Edinburgh would shed some light on Sir William Alexander's place in Scottish political and literary history. While in Edinburgh I was also looking forward to meeting Aonghus MacKenzie, who a friend in Chester, Nova Scotia had told me had a knowledge of Alexander and his times.

I arrived in Edinburgh on a very cold and windy late-January evening just as a winter storm was about to start, and was relieved to get quickly settled into a comfortable and hospitable bed and breakfast within walking distance of the Scottish Record Office, thanks to the help of a city-wise Edinburgh cabby. After dinner, I phoned Aonghus MacKenzie, who insisted I drop by his house just a few blocks away, the next evening, January 25th, to partake of a down-home, Robbie Burns Night celebration.

My first day of archival research in Edinburgh at General Register House, a solid Georgian building designed by one of Scotland's renowned architects, was taken up in registering and acquainting myself with its system for finding appropriate materials. Starkly different from Kew in design, layout, and operation, it offered little in the way of technological aids, but various staff members came to my rescue as I slowly flipped through card indexes and carefully followed file references to their source.

The Guthry letter, which I was eager to read, had been discovered by Naomi Griffiths loosely placed in the back of bound material dealing with the creation of the chivalric order of the Knights-Baronets of Nova Scotia. Sitting with about half-a-dozen other researchers in the building's second-floor long room, I scanned through other related material while an aging assistant fetched the appropriate volume. I hoped that the Richard Guthry letter would still be where Griffiths had found it. It was, and with it was another letter, written by a Robert Angus, describing some of the geography and coastline of early-seventeenth-century Nova Scotia.

The Guthry letter deals in detail with various matters relating to the settlers' departure from England, their arrival in Nova Scotia, and the founding of the settlement. There are interesting observations about the appearance and lifestyle of the Mi'kmaq and the surrounding terrain. In contrast, the Angus letter deals extensively with geographical matters and the bounty of fish and fowl around the province's southern shoreline. Guthry clearly states that he penned his missive at Charlesfort in Port Royal, New Scotland in August of 1629. From a couple of comments in the letter, it is reasonable to conclude that it is addressed to Sir William Alexander himself. Who Guthry was and where he hailed from remains a mystery, but his letter, in period English dialect, contains a smattering of Scottish words along with some Latin and French phrases, indicating quite clearly that he was an educated and, no doubt, valued member of the new settlement. Time passed quickly that day as I acquainted myself with the stylized writing, lingered over strange words, and strained to make sense of the many interconnected sentences. (More on Guthry's letter in a later chapter.)

The day's intense work had me looking forward to a relaxing evening at Aonghus MacKenzie's enjoying the music and poetry of Scotland's "poet of the people." I arrived at the celebrations and was quickly warmed by the contents of a liberal glass of the national brew and introduced to a roomful of avid Burns enthusiasts. It was an enjoyable evening but, because of its nature any serious discussion with Aonghus had to be put off, so we made arrangements to get together later during my Edinburgh stay. The next few days were trying and exhausting, as I tried to keep abreast of my research and fight off a flu virus. I had a two-day wait for the delivery of material from archives elsewhere in the city and was tempted to stay in bed, but I couldn't afford the luxury, as I had only a certain amount of time in Edinburgh before my departure for Stirling and Alexander's birthplace at nearby Menstrie. From there it would be on to Glasgow and a flight back to Canada. I made my way to the Scottish National Portrait Gallery and to the offices of Historic Scotland to view and order slides of Alexander and his Renaissance manor house in Stirling. I was glad to spend a long afternoon inside the National Library, where I found the collected writings of Alexander's close friend and fellow Scottish poet, William Drummond of Hawthornden. Among his collected manuscripts I came across references to the fact that Alexander had offered his diplomatic services and acted as peace negotiator between opposing religious factions at home and in Europe, and that he was particularly active in negotiations between England and the Vatican around 1633, when Charles I was being threatened by political and religious rebellion at home.

Back at the Scottish Record Office a few days later, I happened to come across references to the fact that Sir William's ancestors had been granted Temple lands in Menstrie, and this made me curious as to whether there were any more direct links between the Alexander family and the Order of Knights Templar. Although I had no doubt that there were practical and pecuniary reasons for many of Alexander's pursuits later in life, I wondered if, in his youth growing up in surroundings associated with Templar Knights, he had somehow been introduced to and inspired by some of their ideals and accomplishments. He certainly had close ties later in life with high-ranking members of the emerging Masonic Order, which, according to some sources, carried forward the esoteric Christian philosophy adopted and practiced by the Templars. I expected to find some evidence of this in his writings.

Nursing a sore throat, I spent my last evening in Edinburgh with Aonghus in a local pub listening to him explain, as only a totally unapologetic, fervent Scot could, that the reason Sir William Alexander had never been popular in Scotland was because he had been seen as a lackey of the English and a traitor to the cause of Scottish independence. He had abandoned in his writing his native vernacular in favour of Elizabethan English and had consistently served the political and religious interests of the British Crown, understandable reasons for the insipid support in his native Scotland for his Nova Scotia scheme.

Much to my relief, instead of launching into a nationalist tirade against the idea of writing a book about Alexander, Aenghus courteously suggested I read a recently published Scottish history he recommended, and obliged me with the names of contacts in Stirling, where Alexander had lived for part of his adult life.

Because of bad weather, I had to forgo my planned trip to Stirling and Menstrie. Instead I took the opportunity to recover from my bout with the flu and a few days later I was on a train to Glasgow where I had discussions about Alexander's association with Glasgow University as a student and benefactor.

It was with a sense of both accomplishment and relief that I left the winter winds of Scotland behind and settled into a seat of an Air Canada Boeing 767 for my flight back to Nova Scotia. As the plane headed out over a choppy North Atlantic, my thoughts turned to the courageous souls who had set out centuries earlier in the same direction in wooden ships at the mercy of wind and wave.

Within a couple of weeks of returning to Nova Scotia and after visits to the Archives in Halifax, the Special Collections Department at Acadia University in Wolfville, and meetings with local historians in the Annapolis Royal area, I settled into a rented log house overlooking the rugged southern shore of the Bay of Fundy. Here, in view of the waters over which Alexander's expedition had sailed into the Annapolis Basin, and not far from where the heroic Charlesfort settlers had struggled to survive, I spent the next three months sorting through my notes and writing the story of Sir William Alexander and his connection to Nova Scotia.

4

A Celtic Heritage

My London research into the life and times of Sir William Alexander confirmed that here was a man who had risen from being an obscure poet among the ranks of the lesser nobility to occupy high office in the court of King James I. This was the time when the Crowns of England and Scotland merged, creating the political entity that became known as Great Britain. Alexander played a role in this historic transition, much as he contributed to that other great movement of his time, the westward passage of settlers from both countries to the new world across the Atlantic. An accomplished scholar, he was no less remarkable as a politician. Living in a time of tremendous political and religious change, he faced opposition and hostility while carrying out the responsibilities of his several offices of state. A man of intelligence and integrity, he brought these abilities to bear on the challenges he faced as a Scot serving the commands of an English monarchy. His strength of character and resolute nature were evident in his patient dealings with opposing forces and adverse circumstances and his determination to establish a place in the new world for his fellow countrymen.

Naturally, I was anxious to know more about the background of this extraordinary Scot who, although possibly a Catholic by birth, followed a deeper stream of spirituality than any church of the time could claim. Throughout much of his adult life, Nova Scotia occupied his thoughts and took up much of his energy and resources, but he was never himself to set eyes upon it.

During my sojourn in Scotland I had learned that Sir William Alexander's ancestry reached far back into the misty origins of the Scottish race. Like the race itself, it is a mix of many bloods, including Norse, Irish, Anglo-Norman, and French. It occurred to me that, given his multicultural image, Alexander would feel perfectly at home in the Nova Scotia and Canada of today.

One of the earliest written accounts in Scottish history prior to 100 A.D. was, perhaps not surprisingly, penned by a Roman. It describes the occupying Roman army's last campaign against native rebels north of the Firth of Forth in 83 A.D. (Incidentally, the name of the then Roman Governor of Britain was one that should be quite familiar to present-day Nova Scotians: Agricola Street is one of the main thoroughfares in the city of Halifax.) Setting the trend for the Scots' future passionate preoccupation with militancy and religion, the next written document in the annals of the country's history deals with the life and times of the sixth-century Celtic saint, Columba, and his missionary work in Scotland. For the next 1,000 years and more the forces of warfare and worship, patriotism and prayer, were inextricably inter-woven with the institutions of king and kirk, court and church. Sometimes working together, sometimes apart, they became powerful and predominant elements in the forging of a sense of Scottish nationhood. A strong streak of independence in the blood, geography that generated a sense of place, the threat posed by the land-grabbing English, and an unfettered and indominable Celtic imagination all helped too, of course.

Other episodic events in early Scottish history are known to us only in the remnants of desolate hilltop fortifications that speckle the country's breathtaking landscape and in myriad, almost mythic, accounts of battles and heroes, hermits, and saints. It is for the most part unrecorded history, but history nonetheless.

Ongoing archaeological work at some of these sites, which seems of late to be enjoying the status of a national industry, may shed more light on the nature of early life in Scotland. The unearthing of previously unknown Roman settlements (as has recently occurred in Ireland, through Irish historians long argued the Romans never reached the island) may provide more details about the history of Scotland during the early centuries of Christendom.

A mixture of five distinct peoples who occupied various parts of the country during the first millennium after Christ, the Scots stem, in part, from the Picts who inhabited this wilderness on the northern fringe of the Roman Empire. Given the name *picti* (the "painted people") by a Roman historian, they have often been portrayed as red-haired, large-limbed, and highly combative. Members of loosely connected tribes, they inhabited the lands north of the Forth and Clyde, then known by the Latin name of Caledonia.

In his recent *Scotland, A New History* historian Michael Lynch points out that the precise origin of the Picts is a bit of a mystery, as is the cause of their demise. It is widely assumed that they were at least a remnant of the Celtic root-race of northwestern Europe. That they were a warrior society ruled by warlords, and that they could build ships and were daring seamen, seems beyond doubt.

The *scotti*, who invaded from northern Ireland in the middle of the fifth century following the Roman withdrawal from Britain, provided additional Celtic blood and some much-needed centralized leadership. These "men of Dalriada," as they were known, were apparently as ferocious as the Picts, but possessed greater organizational ability, and they helped forge the first traces of future nationhood in what became known as the ancient Kingdom of Alba. Its first accredited monarch, Kenneth MacAlpin, was crowned around 850 at Scone, a place that would from then on have profound significance for both Scottish royalty and the people of Scotland.

The arrival of the *scotti* from Ireland also brought a transformative and civilizing religious influence. St. Columba was one of those hermitic Irish monks who, following in the tradition of St. Patrick, helped spread Christianity north and west in the sixth century. Columba, or *Colum Cille* as he was known in Gaelic, is thought to be responsible for the development of a distinctively Celtic Christianity in Scotland. This early Christian influence, strengthened by the efforts of Scotland's eleventh-century Queen Margaret and then infused with the religious Reformation of John Knox in the mid-sixteenth century, led to a distinctly national Scottish church. Its royal emblem, the saltired or lengthwise cross of the apostle St. Andrew, forms part of the present flag of Nova Scotia.

Other groups, with their customs and cultures, also contributed to the development of the Scottish race as we know it today. The Britons of the southwest, having been pushed northward by Germanic tribes after the Romans withdrew from England, became part of the mix. Then, in the eighth century, the Norse moved down from Scandinavia and aggressively intruded on part of the mainland and outlying islands to the north and west. Yet, in spite of their diverse cultural backgrounds, their competitive interests in acquiring territory, their inherent hostility to one another, and the fact that they populated different parts of the country, all these various groupings managed to form a loose alliance, if not a united nation, under common leadership by the time Malcolm Canmore claimed the throne of Scotland in 1058.

Malcolm's Scotland was a land of barren mountains and thick forests, riddled with rivers, lakes, and much bog. Its predominantly poorer and more hostile terrain had, since the days of the Roman invasion, left it more isolated than England. Even to the Romans, with all their military might and engineering capabilities, much of Scotland remained an unexplored, rugged wilderness known mostly for its fierce, war-like clansmen. Hunting and fishing, cattle, sheep, and goat herding were the main preoccupations of the population throughout much of the mountainous terrain of the northwest, although more pastoral agricultural practices were probably pursued in the more fertile eastern and southern lowlands. Villages, small clusters of primitive peat-and-stone houses, were few and far between. The only cities, if one could call them that, were fortified settlements on high ground, such as those at Edinburgh and Stirling.

In spite of its early geographic isolation from the European mainland, and perhaps because of it, the country, surrounded as it was by water on three sides, had one geological feature that favoured maritime trade and communication with the outside world, especially to the north and west. These were the firths, the deep coastal inlets that cut into its shoreline, most noticeably in the west, and which since earliest times had encouraged sea travel.

During Malcolm's reign and that of Margaret, his spiritually inclined English wife, Norman political and religious structures such as feudalism and monasticism first began to appear and spread in Scotland. The feudal system of government placed ownership of all land with the king and gave him the right and power to award property to his appointed lords or vassals. These "ward-holding" members of the nobility agreed in turn to serve the king as needed and to come to his aid in times of war. As long as the monarch wasn't an imbecile or despot and the knights remained loyal to their part of the bargain, both parties benefited.

Feudalism was so successfully transplanted to southern and eastern Scotland that by the time of the famous Battle of Bannockburn in 1314, when Scotland inflicted a crushing defeat on the English, King Robert the Bruce's victory was in no small part due to a large contingent of these warrior knights.

Politically, this feudal arrangement was very different in both principle and practice from the hereditary clan system that had previously existed in Scotland to that time. Feudalism, which contrasted sharply with the more localized nature of clan affiliation and loyalty then still dominant in the highlands and the west, succeeded in creating a widely based hierarchical pyramid of power with the monarch at its apex. The king granted land to favoured nobles who in turn "feude" part of their holdings to lesser lords in return for payment in cash or kind. These Scottish "lairds" then rented sections of land to agricultural labourers who lived on and worked the land, most of them at a subsistence level. By their physical labours, the peasants maintained a roof of sorts over their heads, and oatmeal, but little else, on their tables. The fruits of their labours went for the most part to their landlords.

Dressed in long and colourful woollen blankets tied in at the waist (the kilt wasn't invented until the eighteenth century) the peasant possessed few personal effects beyond a cooking pot, plates, cups, knives, and spoons. He and his wife, whose outer clothing amounted to little more than a linen skirt and a shoulder plaid, seldom knew a bed beyond the gatherings of straw sufficient to cushion their bodies against the earthen floor of their mud-and-stone cabin. Oatmeal made into porridge, gruel, or oatbread was the staff of life, supplemented too rarely with fish, shellfish, poultry, milk, and eggs, and, in times of extreme hardship, the blood of living animals. Enough to avoid starvation at the best of times, it inevitably led to serious malnutrition for half the population.

At the other end of the social spectrum, the laird could afford to play the genial host, and was expected to do so under the terms of the feudal arrangement. And so developed a tradition among the nobility of throwing sumptuous banquets where the guests, with typically Celtic hospitality, were regaled by pipers, fiddlers, harpists, and singers. The Scots liked to party prodigiously when occasion and victuals permitted.

European monasticism, with its large, literate, land-holding orders, such as the Benedictines and the Cistercians, were very different from the small hermitic communities developed earlier by St. Columba and his followers. They brought a much-needed sense of disciplined development, common direction, and centralized authority to the rather irregular practices of the more loosely organized and widely scattered Celtic church. They also brought a fresh infusion of religious fervour to the country and further strengthened the relationship between church and court.

Ironically, this relationship would in time lead to a Scottish-born king sitting on the English throne in London and replacing the Pope in Rome as titular head of the church in Scotland. It would also help determine the dominant religious influence in early Nova Scotia.

These European influences, although strongly opposed in the more rugged north and west, were effectively established in the Scottish lowlands, and were strengthened and extended during the reigns of Malcolm's sons. This was especially so in the case of the highly regarded King David I, who ruled Scotland from 1124 to 1153. Educated in the ways of the Anglo-Norman court, where according to one chronicler of the time, he "lost much of his barbarous origins," the holder of an English title and married to an English wife, David brought to the Scottish court a large retinue of European-leaning followers.

Adding to the deepening of Norman influences at court and the extension of Norman practices among the Scottish nobility during David's reign was the marriage of Malcolm's daughter Matilda to the Norman King Henry I of England. It is no surprise that an early-thirteenth-century historian referred to the royal house of Scotland, perhaps with some exaggeration, as "French in race and manner of life, in speech and in culture."

So began the centuries-long, bittersweet saga of conflict and intrigue among the royal households of Scotland, England, and France. It would bring triumph and tragedy, honour and ignominy to some of those directly involved, and affect for hundreds of years the lives of millions of people in all three countries. This struggle would also be played out in Nova Scotia and other territories in the new world.

Naturally, these political and religious developments were not welcomed wholeheartedly by some of the indigenous Scottish lairds and chieftains, especially those in the more rugged west and north. Opposition was at times quite fierce and prolonged. It was around this time that Sir William Alexander's renowned Norse ancestor, Conn Chead Chath, was finally forced to submit to the Scottish throne. As a result of the Norse invasion and conquest of the outlying islands, he had ruled over Mull, Jura, Tiree, Isla, Bute, and even Kintyre, and was considered a king in his own right. For a time, he created what amounted to a second royal house in Scotland in his Celtic western stronghold. Because of this family's support of the territorial claims of Robert the Bruce in the late-thirteenth century,

a close relationship was established with the monarchy, which resulted in the marriage of John, a later Lord of the Isles, and Margaret,
daughter of King Robert II, the first of the Stewart line of kings, who
ruled Scotland from 1371 to 1390. Their third son was named Alexander, and his son Turloch was awarded lands in Argyllshire.

During the reign of King Robert III, another branch of the same
family, the powerful western-based Campbell clan also known as the
Earls of Argyll, had been granted extensive lands in Clackmannan-
shire east of the the royal stronghold of Stirling. Here they built
Castle Campbell, strategically situated high above Dollar Glen,
which afforded both a commanding view of the surrounding countryside and convenient access to the royal court. It was from their
powerful Campbell cousins that the Alexanders acquired their land
at Menstrie.

Nestled below the low-lying Ochil Hills, the village of Menstrie
lies just a few kilometres east of the strategically positioned and
majestic Stirling Castle. It is also just north of the winding Forth and
the twelfth-century Augustinian monastery at Cambuskenneth. To
the south lies the battlefield of Bannockburn, where Robert the Bruce
won his resounding victory over the invading English forces of
Edward II in June of 1314. At Menstrie, in surroundings rich in both
pastoral beauty and patriotic landmarks, the Alexanders built a mod-
est Norman castle early in the sixteenth century.

Menstrie Castle

In records relating to the abbey at Cambuskenneth, there is reference to one of William Alexander's more immediate predecessors residing in the area. A Thomas Alexander of Menstrie is recorded as having acted in March of 1506 as one of a number of assessors in a boundary dispute between the abbey and Sir David Bruce of Clackmannan. Later moves by the powerful, land-rich Argylls gave his sons additional holdings. Other records show that on August 25, 1529 the family entered into a feudal agreement with their Campbell cousins whereby they were given possession of the farmlands, mill, and bog at Menstrie in exchange for an annual payment of, among other things, 24 bolls of wheat, 24 bolls of oats, 5 unsheared sheep, and 52 capons.

One aspect of the family's early land holdings especially interested me. Among land registrations on file in the Scottish Public Records Office in Edinburgh there is reference to the Alexanders inheriting Temple lands at Menstrie in 1537 and again in 1553. Yet another reference confirms that the family still held Temple lands some twenty years later. These transactions may be an indication of some family connection, perhaps through the Campbells, to the famed medieval religious order of the Knights Templar of the Order of St. John of Jerusalem, which had among its number members of the Scottish nobility. The Order is known to have been granted land in Scotland where, during the thirteenth century, it established a headquarters at Balantrodoch, now simply called Temple, just south of Edinburgh. Many Temple properties reverted back to Scottish families during this period and it seems that this is how the Alexander family acquired their Temple lands.

This indirect link between the Alexander household and the mysterious Templars became all the more interesting when I learned of the later involvement of at least two of Sir William Alexander's sons with Scottish Freemasonry early in the seventeenth century. (Some Masonic historians associate their fraternity with the Templars.) Equally fascinating was my discovery in the library of the Masonic Grand Lodge in Halifax that, according to the late Reginald Harris, a highly respected Halifax lawyer and a former Grand Master and Grand Historian of Freemasons in Nova Scotia, the order may have been active in Alexander's Charlesfort. More about the implications and ramifications of this in a later chapter.

William Alexander was likely born in 1567 or soon afterwards, the only son of an Alexander Alexander and his wife Marion. Although birth records for the parish of Logie, of which Menstrie was part, have long since been lost, various sources suggest 1567 as the most likely date. Little or nothing is known about his earliest years other than they were spent in the peaceful confines of Menstrie Castle. When his father died in early 1581, he and two sisters were left in the charge of his granduncle, James Alexander, a well-placed Burgess of Stirling. Alexander's boyhood years were spent in that ancient and historic city surrounded by the regal sights and sounds of its renowned castle.

Such was the political, social and religious background to the family and formative years of Sir William Alexander.

5

Renaissance Learning

It is generally believed that the man who devoted much of his life to creating a New Scotland in North America received his first formal education at the grammar school in Stirling where, from his first day, he would have had to follow strict rules and a stringent round of studies in an atmosphere conditioned by the dominant church teachings of the time. His teacher was probably Thomas Buchanan, nephew of the celebrated scholar and historian George Buchanan. The elder Buchanan had been tutor to Prince James, son of the tragically fated Mary Queen of Scots and future King of both Scotland and England. Alexander's early education laid the foundations for his future classical studies, literary pursuits, and life at court. Perhaps it was during these early years of rigid scholasticism that Alexander acquired his strong religious faith and those streaks of determination and patient perseverance in the face of opposition and overwhelming odds that he displayed later in life. Growing up in his uncle's house in the company of his sisters, we can only assume that he enjoyed a warm and supportive family environment.

William Alexander grew up during a most dramatic and turbulent period of Scottish history in a city dominated by Stirling Castle, one of Scotland's great fortresses, on which the safety of the kingdom had often depended. Situated to straddle the route between the lowlands and highlands, it had, through the centuries, been occupied several times by invading English forces, who considered its possession essential to their dominance of Scotland. In sight of its walls William Wallace led the Scots to a famous victory over the English, who later scornfully displayed from the same walls his dismembered body as a warning to other would-be insurgents.

With its ornamental interiors and its magnificent hall and chapel, Stirling Castle was a Renaissance palace that had long been a favourite abode of Stewart monarchs and their queens. Over the years its walls had heard not only the laughter and music of court banquets and the birth cries of royal infants but also the malicious words of court conspirators and the whisperings of political intrigue and treason. James V of Scotland brought his French bride Mary of Guise there, and their small daughter Mary, the future queen, was carefully guarded there against the treacherous intrigues of England's Henry VIII. It was to Stirling that she returned after her exile in France as the popularly acclaimed Mary Queen of Scots. After being crowned King, James VI of Scotland made Stirling his home, so during Alexander's early years the city was a place of pomp, pageantry, and international influence. This was a fitting early backdrop for one who was to walk through regal halls, hold high office at court, and become a close confidant to two kings of England and Scotland.

Due to its geographic isolation, its historically defensive outlook, its less integrated social fabric, and the extremes of religious reform, Scotland was more hesitant than many other countries to respond to the humanizing and liberating influences of the European Renaissance. Nevertheless, since the time of the remarkable King James IV, Renaissance ideals and ideas in art, architecture, literature, and philosophy had been evident in the Scottish courts of the Stewarts. They invited European artists, poets, sculptors, and men of letters to build, decorate, adorn, lecture, and teach within the realm. This rebirth of classical thought and perception, however, took a long time to penetrate lower levels of a severely repressed society. But by the time of young William Alexander's schooling, the education of even a minor member of the Scottish establishment had a distinct Renaissance tinge. Educated Scots were encouraged, like their counterparts on the continent, to learn to read, write, and speak classical Latin and to study ancient Greek and Roman cultures, whose architects, philosophers, and playwrights were held in high regard.

The European Renaissance, having surfaced at a time when there was much disillusion with the corrupt and exploitive behaviour of the all-powerful established church, with its dogmatic medieval theology divorced from the realities of everyday life of the millions of the faithful, had resulted in an exploration into the mysteries of Eastern mysticism and the long-abandoned precepts of early Christianity. There was a revival of interest in the appealing writings of the early church fathers, and in Plato, with his philosophy of the harmony of the universe and its close relationship to the physical and moral constitution of mankind. This, in turn, gave rise to academies that sought to integrate the ancient teachings of Hermes, Pythagerous, and Zoroaster with Christian thought and where "learned ignorance" or "conscious innocence" were aspired to. Such societies as freemasonry and Rosicrucianism found fertile ground for their new ideas. Proponents of the new thinking, of course, faced persecution by the mainstream political and religious powers of the day, and many paid a high price. The great Italian philosopher Giordano Bruno, who had taught openly in England in 1585, was one of several on the continent burned at the stake by the reactionary forces of orthodoxy for their outspoken insights. But the minds of many had been opened and new light filtered into the dark corners of medieval thought. In spite of the risks involved, the human spirit was moving knowledgeably and forcefully everywhere — in art, literature, philosophy, religion, and science. In England, the new thinking was embraced by poets and courtiers, and by the years of Alexander's early education, it had swept into Scotland as well.

Renaissance thought brought the romantic music of Italy and the art of France into the previously bleak and austere dwellings of Scottish nobles, whose castles and manors were now beginning to reflect more decorative European tastes in architecture. But this reawakening of human awareness was not defined solely by the interests and actions of aesthetes, artists, poets, and philosophers. Europeans were literally on the move and trans-Atlantic adventurism and exploration were opening up a new world that would test the mettle of the continent's more daring seamen, risk-taking merchants, and imaginative statesmen.

Paralleling the spread of Renaissance thinking in Scotland was the religious Reformation, which was given popular impetus in Germany by Martin Luther in the early-sixteenth century and was soon extended northwards by John Calvin. The Roman Catholic church, which had dominated Europe for centuries had, in the minds of many, become intolerably corrupt. There had been mounting concern even within the church itself that it was neglecting its true purpose — the spiritual education and pastoral care of the people — by its focus on the perpetuation of its material power. Abuses were openly cited by Luther and others, and by the middle of the sixteenth century almost half of Europe had rejected both the supremacy of the papacy and the validity of certain church practices, particularly the mass. The Reformation was a justifiable call for a return to basic goodness, to justice, charity, and love. However, Martin Luther's vision was further radicalized by the French-born cleric John Calvin, who set up his headquarters in Geneva. In Scotland's religious zealot John Knox, authoritarian and puritanical religion found one of its staunchest and most vociferous champions. In time, Knox's firebrand fundamentalism gave rise to that unique form of church worship and government, Scottish Presbyterianism.

The Reformation-influenced Scottish Parliament of 1560 abolished Catholicism and, following the example set by Henry VIII in England, established Protestantism as the official religion of the country. However the more extreme Scottish Protestant movement set out to establish the church, the "kirk," as the supreme authority over the state, rather than as in England, the other way around.

In spite of Knox's fear-mongering sermons calling for the new and narrower moral code as contained in his *Book of Discipline*, at least half of the Scottish nobility remained loyal to Rome. Although sympathetic to the Protestant cause, the nobility as a whole had no intention of handing over civic power, control of the universities, and the enormous wealth of the church to a new militant priesthood led by the politically astute Knox.

Nonetheless, the kirk openly declared that it alone should legislate on morals and prescribe penalties for everything from adultery to the worship of "false images of idolatry," such as pictures and statues of saints. It even went so far as to suggest that all who persistently ignored or resisted its strict code should be put to death. Knox's expressed concern for the spiritual welfare of the Scottish people was given a highly charged political edge in his repeated denouncements of court life and his loudly expressed perception of its corrupting influence on the rest of society. His moralistic outrage was further fuelled by the fact that the thrones of both Scotland and England were occupied by spirited and intelligent women, both of whom he was at pains to publicly denounce as "whores and Jezebels".

All this rampant political and religious turmoil made the days of Alexander's youth a heady time. Although enrollment records from the period are lost, it is certain he attended Glasgow University, as the fact is mentioned by several contemporary sources. The fact that he later took a particular interest in the welfare of that university and that, according to existing records, seven of his eight sons attended Glasgow, also strongly suggest it was his alma mater. There are also references to his having attended Leyden, the Dutch university frequented by many young Scottish nobles of his time, although there is no documented evidence that he took a degree there. Certainly the extensive classical learning he later displayed in his writings support the theory that he received the kind of higher education pursued by young members of the aristocracy and lesser nobility of the day.

Apart from his early teacher, Thomas Buchanan, there was at least one other strong intellectual influence in his life. At some point he formed a friendship with Alexander Hume, a Paris-educated Scottish lawyer who, like his French counterpart Marc Lescarbot, sought a more stable and meaningful life away from the combativeness of the legal profession and the superficialities of court life. Hume, who turned to theology and became a minister in the parish of Logie, was also a writer and associated with prominent literary figures of his day. As is so often the case in friendships of this kind, the older Hume may have acted as a mentor of sorts and his influence may have encouraged the young Alexander to pursue the literary avenues he did early in his career.

Alexander passed his teenage years at a time when English came into its own as a language capable of expressing great dramatic themes and poetic flights of fancy, as demonstrated by writers such as Philip Sidney, Edmund Spenser, Christopher Marlowe, Ben Jonson, and William Shakespeare. Of course, they and others owed a debt to the classical poets and dramatists of ancient Greece and Rome, as well as more recent French and Italian translators and imitators. But by their determination to express themselves in the language of their own country, they created the Elizabethan literary Renaissance. Alexander, who was reputed to have begun composing poetry in Stirling at the age of fifteen, aspired to be part of it.

As a young man in his early twenties, having gained a reputation as one who was both scholarly and talented, Alexander was chosen by his powerful and well-connected Campbell cousins to accompany their son, the seventh Earl of Argyle, on the then customary Grand Tour, an educational trip around Europe undertaken by many sons of the nobility. By following the trend of the time, and the advise of the French genius Montaigne — that travel was an important part of a good education provided one kept one's eyes and ears open and left one's prejudices at home — these youngbloods from the coarse and chilly north broadened their intellectual horizons with a taste of the exotic in the warmer countries across the English Channel. Alexander's tour introduced him to the prevailing manners of European courts, helped him improve his knowledge of other languages, and acquainted him first-hand with the factors and factions of the European artistic and political scene. It must have helped prepare him for his future work as a courtier, peace negotiator, and elder statesman. His sojourn through France, Italy, and Spain also had the more immediate effect of prompting his Celtic soul into composing passionate love poems, earning him a reputation as a sonneteer.

When Alexander and his cousin walked into the open university that was Italy, their northern sensibilities probably responding eagerly to its scenery, music, women, and wine, it had long been the reservoir from which flowed the creative spirit of the Renaissance. It was also the power centre of the Christian world. In its many palaces and multitude of churches the young Scots saw the works of the country's renowned artists. In its lecture halls they might have heard the new ideas advanced by men such as Galileo and Bruno, and in its public places viewed the architectual masterpieces of Michelangelo and Palladio. Italy had also produced celebrated poets such as Ariosto and Tasso, whose works no doubt interested the young Alexander. Along with the classical plays of ancient Greece and Rome, its theatres offered romantic pastoral dramas set in the legendary kingdom of Arcadia. Able and adventurous Italian seamen had navigated the Atlantic and charted the coastline of a new continent.

In Spain, Alexander was exposed to the grandeur of what had recently been the richest and most powerful empire of his time and felt the pervading aura of piety perpetuated by its austere monarch, Phillip II. From Madrid, he may have journeyed to see the architectural wonder that was the Escorial, part royal palace, part religious community. Spanish architecture offered a feast for the eyes, and its elaborate creations testified to the wealth and taste of the ruling aristocracy and the power of the church. Supported by the seemingly unending supply of gold and silver from its American conquests over the previous century, Spain had sought to expand its power as the self-appointed protector of medieval Roman Catholicism, but costly wars with the Turks, French Protestants known as Huguenots, and Protestants in the Netherlands had taken their toll on both the inflated Spanish economy and the nation's psyche. Once the dominant sea power in Europe, the ignominious defeat of its seemingly invincible Armada against England deprived Spain of some of its former glory. In a countryside that had become increasingly unproductive as a result of years of Spanish military adventure, the young Alexander may have quietly reflected on the growing poverty of the peasantry, which had little to console itself with other than excesses of devotion, bullfights, and passionate music. Nonetheless, it was still a self-contained country with a reputation for chivalry and courtly manners that together with its language, attracted those adventurous enough to cross its borders in pursuit of an Iberian dimension to their education.

Spain adopted a seige mentality that left it relatively untouched by the liberating humanism of the Renaissance. Even so, it remained a land of much learning, peppered with scholastic minds, numerous universities, and an irrepressible creative spirit. Here was the haunting religious art of El Greco and the imaginative landscape of Don Quixote, whose creator, Cervantes, changed the temper of Spanish literature with one book. In light of modern psychological knowledge, we can now understand how, in spite of fierce sexual suppression and religious censorship, Spain was also the home of a raucous theatre that produced the ribald and romantic dramas of De Vega.

However, France probably left the strongest impression on Alexander during his travels and likely was of greatest interest to him. Long the friendly ally of Scotland, its history for years had been closely associated with that of his native land through royal marriages and international trade.

By 1590, the French countryside was recovering from the widespread chaos and devastation caused by years of internal religious conflict highlighted by the horrors of the St. Bartholomew's Day massacre in 1572, when up to 30,000 Huguenots were mercilessly put to death. Alexander must have learned early about the horrific consequences of religious extremism, especially when used for political ends, something he was to come face-to-face with in his own land later in life.

During the first half of the sixteenth century, France under King Francis I had boasted of both a magnificent court and a powerful army. Although envied and admired by other European rulers due to his military power and the splendour of his palaces, Francis' achievements were accomplished only by means of heavy taxation and political control of extensive and remunerative church properties. His unapologetic control over the Catholic church in France gave him the power to appoint bishops and other clergy throughout the realm. Luther's Reformation, though popular in Germany, had yet to take hold to any great degree in France. This mutually agreeable bedding down of church and state was, however, eventually challenged by dedicated followers of France's own home-grown religious reformer, John Calvin. His ideas about reforming church government proved attractive to dissident French political and social groups, and by the time Henri II arrived on the throne in 1547 the Reformation was widespread. Encouraged by preachers from Calvin's headquarters in Geneva and helped by the development of printing and the translation of the Bible, secret study groups were meeting in private homes. The movement grew to become a threat to the established church. Political instability mounted due to opposition to the monarchy by the powerful Guise family, which made its own claims to the throne. By about 1550, France was a hotbed of warring factions supporting opposing family claims to the throne, and was engulfed in open conflict between militant Huguenots and the Catholic majority.

Henri II was killed in a jousting accident in 1559, and Calvin's followers, interpreting this as a sign from God, came out into the open and began to hold public meetings. Within months of Henri's death, a general synod was held in Paris and hundreds of prominent citizens rallied to the Protestant cause. By the early 1560s there were at least 2,000 Huguenot congregations in the country and the reformed faith was firmly established as a religious and political force in French society.

At this point, the connection between the royal households of France and Scotland began to influence the destinies of both nations. Henri's immediate successor, Francis II, died within a year of assuming the throne, which left his attractive eighteen-year-old Scottish-born wife Mary, the daughter of King James V of Scotland, free to pursue other interests. These included the throne of her native land. Her son by a later marriage would eventually become King of England and issue Sir William Alexander his charter to settle Nova Scotia.

Francis II was succeeded by his ten-year-old brother, the emotionally unstable and unpredictable Charles IX, who, because of his tender years, was dominated politically and personally by his mother, Catherine de Medici, for many years. With a wisdom born of many years of experience as a skillful power broker, Catherine sought a peaceful compromise with the country's Huguenot minority. It seemed a reasonable solution might be found, but in 1562 the Guise family initiated a civil war of sorts, unleashing a bloody terror across the country that led to the carnage of Saint Bartholomew's Day in 1572.

It was not until 1594 that a welcome peace brought 32 years of almost continual conflict to an end. It was the intellectually emancipated, romantically inclined, but war-weary Henri of Navarre who made this possible. Much to the surprise of his Huguenot supporters, he converted to Catholicism while laying siege to Paris, the final prize in the civil war. When he ascended the throne as Henri IV, the country's economy, food supply, and cultural life were quickly stabilized. Simple of manner, speech, and attire, and possessing high intelligence and a disarming sense of humour, Henri proved to be perhaps the most humane of all French kings. His concern for the welfare of his subjects made France once again a pleasant and hospitable place in which to live. He instituted new and efficient agricultural methods, using Crown lands to demonstrate good husbandry practices. He took measures to protect the peasantry from military abuse and to safeguard their crops from careless destruction. The French countryside quickly returned to a state of productivity. He initiated public works projects in an all-out effort to alleviate the widespread unemployment of his time. Parks and squares were laid out, trees were planted, and canals were dug as civic pride grew and the economy improved. He enacted radical management-labour relations policies that encouraged the development of various crafts and made France a leading European manufacturer of exceptionally fine pottery and glass. Equally important, he astutely and diplomatically maintained peace between the country's long-feuding Catholics and Huguenots.

These were no small accomplishments, especially in view of the preceding decades of conflict. Henri IV also set Frenchmen's sights once again on the prospect of establishing themselves in a New France across the Atlantic. While in France, Alexander may have learned something about the colonies France had tried in vain to establish many years earlier on the North American continent. In 1603, Henri IV granted a ten-year charter to Sieur de Monts, giving him leave to explore and establish a trading settlement in Acadie. By a rather strange twist of fate, one of the prominent members of this early French colony known as Port Royal, the tenacious French trader Claude de La Tour, would prove to be of great assistance years later to Sir William Alexander and the members of the Charlesfort settlement.

To Alexander of Menstrie, France must have been both intellectually fascinating and sensually stimulating. He was probably appropriately impressed by the highly mannered, glamourous life of a French court now restored to its former brilliance and by the reviving cultural life of the nation. Under an able administration made up of members of both the existing aristocracy and a rising middle class of lawyers and other professionals, the arts flowered once again. Poets and playwrights prospered in the creative environment of Henri's France. As an aspiring writer, Alexander may have participated in literary discussions in that uniquely French cultural institution known as *le salon*. He may have attended productions of classical dramas modelled on the early Roman dramatist and humanist philosopher Seneca, so much in vogue at the time. Once back home in Scotland, Alexander turned his hand to writing plays in the Senecan form, for which he gained quite a reputation.

Although no known personal records exist of his time abroad, other than a few hints in his *Aurora* love poems, we can safely assume that his intellect was improved, his tastes refined, and his soul stirred, as they were intended to be, by his European travels. Certainly the experience seems to have been an enjoyable and fruitful one, for in 1598 his erstwhile travelling companion, the Earl of Argyle, invested Alexander with additional land near Menstrie. A few years later Alexander was given the entire barony of Menstrie by the Earl in consideration of, among other things, services rendered to the Earl "in foreign nations and at home."

Being kinsmen to the Argyles not only brought Alexander additional land grants around Menstrie: the relationship also resulted in his ready access to the Scottish court at Holyrood Palace and the introduction of the promising young poet and budding scholar to King James VI. The historic meeting was to result in both rewarding and disheartening consequences for Alexander over the years, and would link his name forever to part of the then little-explored coast of eastern Canada.

Alexander's intellectual and creative abilities were much admired by the Scottish King, who professed an interest in matters philosophical and welcomed the young Alexander to his court in Edinburgh, where his breeding and his classical education were put to good use. He was given the influential position of tutor to Prince Henry, the King's eldest son and heir to the throne. Once in royal favour, William's disposition, combined with his learning and his dedication to his appointed task, marked him as one whose fortunes would rise in the ensuing years. When King James VI of Scotland moved onto the more powerful English throne as James I in 1603, Alexander followed.

But the responsibilities and demands of his life at court did not cause Alexander to neglect his talents as a poet and playwright. London, with its thriving literary scene, seemed to prompt him to write and publish his major works.

6

The Pen, Not The Sword

To appreciate Alexander's aspirations and achievements as a poet and playwright it is necessary to take into account certain dominant currents and events in the literary and political history of Scotland prior to his birth and during his developing years. Earlier Stewart kings had written poetry, and James VI maintained the traditional family relationship with the muse. More than just a benefactor, he considered himself a teacher of poets. At the time, native poets and their art needed all the help they could get, for a severe blight covered the poetic landscape of this northern nation. With his appointment to court, Alexander found himself in Edinburgh where Holyrood Palace was the centre of power, prestige, and pageantry and where the arts were favoured and flourished.

Unfortunately, with one or two notable exceptions, the poet's pen lay mostly idle across the land. With Scotland's turbulent early history, the aggressive nature of opposing groups claiming territorial rights within its borders, and the constant need for Scots to defend themselves against a better organized and more powerful neighbour to the south, the sword, axe, club, or anything else that might deal an enemy a fatal blow was always close at hand. Among the diverse geographic groupings that made up the emerging Scottish nation, retaliation and revenge became part of the clan code of honour. In time, they solidified into cultural characteristics and, as might be expected of an invaded and oppressed people, a matter of national pride. Consequently, inter-clan disputes could easily escalate into blood feuds and became widespread and generational. That Scotland today lies riddled with the ruins of so many early military strongholds and fortified medieval castles is due in no small part to the fractious and militant nature of early Scottish society. Those who could built highly defensible dwellings, sturdily built structures designed as fortresses to fend off attack from a previously wronged or overly aggressive neighbour, of which there were always many in Scotland.

For nearly 200 years after James I of Scotland, who had developed into a poet of note during his eighteen-year captivity in England, came to the throne in 1424, successive monarchs had tried to bring an end to these destructive inter-clan rivalries. During his reign there was a steady flow of ink from men of letters and a distinctive Scottish voice emerged in the ensuing literature. But the highly divisive internal warfare that had been so much a part of early Scottish history was still a factor in the country during the late sixteenth century. Coupled as it was with intermittent invasions from England and the rise of the Scottish Reformation, there was naturally a good deal of social upheaval that was hardly conducive to the cultivation and flowering of poetry.

Following the death of Scotland's James V, who gave up the ghost in 1542 after suffering disastrous and humiliating defeat at the hands of the better organized and more determined forces of England's Henry VIII at Solway Moss, factions within the Scottish nobility became embroiled in struggles for survival and supremacy. Some favoured the traditional Catholic religion and the centuries-old links with France and Rome, while others advocated reformation of the church, and a Protestant religious alliance with the old enemy, England. No artistic Renaissance could emerge in the midst of such widespread unrest.

After James V's death, his widow, Mary of Guise-Lorraine, ruled as a Catholic monarch with the help of loyal nobles, much to the chagrin of the Calvinist clergy. Matters came to a head following an inflammatory sermon given on May 11, 1559 against the Catholic church and state abuses by John Knox, the self-styled patriarch and leading voice of a severe Scottish Protestantism. Riots and revolution spread as the Lords of the Faithful Congregation, a consolidation of die-hard Calvinists and disillusioned nobles, rose in open opposition to the policies and practices of the Catholic Crown.

During the same year, the late King's young daughter, also named Mary, became the glamorous young Queen of France after a diplomatically arranged marriage to the equally young King Francis II. All seemed rosy and romantic for the young royal couple and the "auld alliance" between the two nations seemed as secure as ever. But, just eighteen months later Francis was dead of a suspicious ear infection, leaving his childless bride to mourn her loss, ponder on the vicissitudes of fate, and plan her personal and political future alone.

In August of 1561, after being courted by members of the Scottish nobility and encouraged by the prompting of her mother, Mary returned to a triumphant coronation in Edinburgh to sit on the throne as the youthful and glamorous Mary Queen of Scots. Regrettably, she had no personal knowledge of the Scottish political scene into which she had entered, but her first years on the throne were something of a political honeymoon. Following well-placed advice she avoided any excess of religious opinion or political action that might have plunged the country into turmoil. She occupied herself with such matters as achieving financial stability for both Crown and country and with visiting, with as little pomp as possible, various parts of her new realm. However, in the militant, male-dominated, and unsettled domain in which she found herself Queen, the fact that she was a woman, displayed a passionate nature, was Catholic, and had French sympathies did not bode well for her future. She maintained a private chapel at Holyrood where she attended daily Mass, much to the disgutst of her many Protestant opponents. She had brought a French entourage of personal attendants with her from France and once on the throne she imported and promoted European tastes in the arts, fashion, and food. Poetry, especially the poetry of love, had a place at Mary's court, which further inflamed the extremist Knox and other narrow-minded divines who were convinced that this attractive and vibrant woman with her French ways was bewitching the men of Scotland and leading the country to hellfire and damnation.

In 1565 Mary married the young, handsome, hard-drinking, and unpredictable Lord Darnley, to whom she had become attracted after nursing him through a severe illness. She had already refused a number of more appropriate suitors, including an assortment of European kings and princes of varying ages. Nine months after their wedding and to the horror of his pregnant wife, who witnessed the terrible event in her private quarters, Darnley participated in the brutal stabbing death of her close friend, David Riccio. Also murdered that night was the Queen's Dominican friar and advisor, John Black. It is hard to know what motivated Darnley's action, but there was certainly mounting resentment among members of the Protestant nobility to Mary's Catholic associates and their influence at court. Darnley may have taken part in the murder of a possible rival for his wife's affections in order to gain support for his own independent rule. Three months after the terrible murder, Mary gave birth to an infant son, the future James VI of Scotland and James I of England, the man who would in time favour the young poet from Menstrie, William Alexander.

Outside Edinburgh, in February of 1567, Darnley was himself murdered after the house he was in was blown up. Suspicion naturally focused on Mary, and it only increased after she married her influential administrator, the Earl of Bothwell, within three months of Darnley's death. By mid-June, the couple were in the hands of revolutionaries known as the Confederate Lords. Bothwell was sent into exile in Denmark where he died in prison, while Mary was forced to abdicate in favour of her infant son. The new king, James VI, was crowned at Stirling Castle in July 1567. He was all of thirteen months old.

Argyll's Lodgings or Stirling Castle

An artist's impression of Argyll's Lodgings

The young King had been baptized a Catholic and was crowned at Stirling in a ceremony obviously designed to be as ecumenical as possible. It included John Knox as preacher and was performed, not in the royal chapel, but in the parish church of the Holy Rood. While still a boy, James was placed under the guardianship of the Erskines, hereditary keepers of Stirling Castle and the family William Alexander would later marry into.

In spite of its early promise, the six-year reign of Scotland's young Renaissance Queen ended with the country caught up in civil war. Mary soon escaped from her forced confinement, precipitating five years of fighting in which the two main rival families were the Hamiltons and the Douglases. Left with little option but to abandon her well-protected young son, Mary managed to cross into England where she remained, usually in a state of refined captivity, until her eventual execution some twenty years later.

In the meantime, Scotland was ruled by a series of regents, men appointed to rule the realm in place of the child monarch. As might be expected, two of them were assassinated as a matter of political expediency and efficiency. Scottish parliaments of this period pursued a pattern of reciprocal land grabs, forfeitures of goods, and executions. A religious ferocity fuelled family rivalries and intensified the conflict. The war came to an end in 1572 with the fall of Edinburgh Castle to an English artillery bombardment. Victory, ironically enough, was won by an alliance of the King's men and advocates of a reformed Scottish church.

In June 1581, after the execution of the regent, the Earl of Morton, on a politically motivated charge of treason, the country was thrown once again into a state of political turmoil. Scotland was close to the brink of yet another civil war when, in August 1582, a group of disgruntled nobles and radical Protestants staged a palace coup. Led by the Earl of Gowrie, they captured and imprisoned the young King and took control of government.

In June of the following year, the King, probably with some inside help, escaped, and the rebels were forced to flee, many to England. This incident was to form the basis of one of William Alexander's first prose pieces. Entitled *A Short Discourse of the Good Ends of Providence in the Late Attempt against His Majesty's Person*, it exhorted the King to pursue the perpetuators of his imprisonment "as miners follow the signs every way as they find in the ground, till they be brought to the body and trunk of the metal." *A*

Short Discourse also showed the young Alexander's loyalty to the King, his willingness to use his pen to reach the royal ear, and a knowledge of and interest in mining.

With the young King now free, laws were passed subjecting all estates and the internal political structure of the reformed church to the authority of the Crown and parliament. When, at the age of nineteen, James VI took control of the reins of power in 1585, there was a reasonably stable central government in place that was loyal to the monarchy. However, Scottish society was still in a state of agitation caused by many years of administrative turmoil, economic instability, and religious unrest.

Outside the principal centres under the control of the King's forces, clans continued to fight over lands, personal slights, favouritism, and anything else they had a mind to. As might be expected, Alexander's family was itself caught up in these feuds and conflicts. Although most tended to be local in origin, some inter-clan clashes, because of the network of allegiances built up over the centuries, became regional mini-wars. In 1590, clan conflict broke out involving the Gordons, the Mackintoshes, the Camerons, and Alexander's cousins, the Campbells. A few years later, the Earl of Argyle, Alexander's patron and the head of the Campbells, took up his sword against the Earl of Huntley, the head of the Gordon clan, following a fierce political squabble. Open warfare broke out between the two families and their associates and took on the proportions of civil war through much of the northern mainland until the Campbell camp was defeated by Huntley, who in turn had to submit to the forces of the Crown.

These feuds were not all highland shenanigans. In spite of the closeness of the central government and the forces of law and order, it was the same story in the lowlands, where, in one instance, Alexander's future in-laws, the Erskines, were in the thick of a bitter and bloody boundary dispute near Stirling. It was much the same, if not worse, in the border area itself, where burning and killing were often used to settle arguments and accounts. Here the problem was exacerbated by the English, who undertook cross-border raids, sometimes in retaliation for previous Scottish intrusions.

One clan chieftain of the time was described as "a very virile man who actively burnt and harried the countryside of his enemy." The outcome of a MacLeod attack in western Ross was typical of the brutality and the destruction experienced in other places. A report of the devastation stated that "Neither man, wife, bairn, house, cover or bigging [outbuilding] had been spared, but all are barbarously slain, burnt and destroyed."

This continuation of centuries-old rivalries among various clans led a distraught and peaceable James VI to later comment that the nobles of Scotland absorbed with their nurses' milk the notions that they must force to submission all those weaker than themselves, that they should defend their own in any wrong regardless of the law, and resort to "banging it out bravely" to the bitter end. Early in his reign James VI, in a treatise on wise kingship called *Basilikon Doron*, addressed to his eldest son and heir Henry, wrote the following advice: "Rest not until ye roote out these barbarous feidesà their barbarous name is unknown to any other nation."

James well knew that the feuding of the lairds was a blight on the nation and, during his remaining years in Scotland prior to his departure for London and the crown of England in 1603, he set his mind and resources to the task of trying to eliminate it. He was not entirely successful.

Such was the state of the country when Alexander returned from Europe. In spite of his cultural conditioning and the involvement of his close relatives and benefactors, the Campbells, in inter-clan warfare, he never showed an inclination to take up the sword alongside them. Having decided to serve the muse, he had put his hand to pen instead.

It was during his travels through Europe that Alexander is believed to have written many of the songs, sonnets, and madrigals published a few years later under the title *Aurora*. This was a time of the great flowering of the English language in both poetry and drama, while in Scotland these art forms had suffered greatly from the repressive attitudes and strict laws of the religious reformers who wished to do away with "the profane and unprofitable art of poem making." Alexander's early education had introduced him to French and Italian poets, and his exposure to the culture of these countries during his travels sparked his spirit into poetic expression. He drew from European and English sources and owed little to the literary traditions of the land of his birth. The influences that moulded him as a writer and show in his collected works were continental and classical. He didn't write as a nationalist or in the national tongue and this perhaps explains in part why his writings received so little recognition among his fellow countrymen and why a contemporary once wrote that Scotland was too small for his talent, which was more suited to a "new world."

Of course, the Scottish balladeers, with their colourful comments on everything from acts of local heroism to national events, maintained a tradition that went back to medieval times and, in their own way, they maintained a distinctively Scottish form of poetry. However, the social upheaval caused by the Reformation and the unstable political state of the country greatly discouraged and diminished the written arts during the latter half of the sixteenth century. The stream of native Scottish poetry almost dried up, and would not swell again until the appearance of Robert Burns nearly two centuries later.

For Alexander, it was perhaps only natural, especially in view of his education, the Renaissance nature of the court, and the literary explosion to the south, that he would adapt his poetry to the English language and its popular form, the sonnet. Imported from France and Italy and popularized in England by Sir Philip Sidney and later by Shakespeare, the sonnet quickly caught on in literary circles. Alexander also used another innovative poetic form imported from Italy, the madrigal, a short love poem that could be sung without musical accompaniment. Most of Alexander's early poems were full of the chivalric romanticism and mild eroticism of the time. He himself would later admit that they contained "the first fancies of the author's youth," and like the early work of some of his more famous English contemporaries who were also very much influenced by the continentals, they are appropriately Italianate. Whatever else he may have learned on his Grand Tour, there is no doubt that Alexander picked up a few pointers on the poetic language of love.

Although he publicly dedicated *Aurora* to the charming Lady Agnes Douglas, later Countess of Argyle and wife of the man who had travelled with him through Europe, the sentiments contained in it are believed to have been addressed to another, older woman, whom some have suggested was Elizabeth Shaw, a neighbour's daughter. Whoever she was, she did not respond to Alexander's initial expressions of interest.

Aurora speaks of a pure but passionate love that is never responded to by the object of the poet's undying affection. Its poems are presented as a sequential description of the varying fortunes of love. The collection begins with Alexander's acknowledgement of the special qualities of his beloved and his inability to express his feelings to her. In the highly stylized and mannered mode of the time, his poems have all the innocence and unsophisticated ardour of a lovesick youth. Here we get a glimpse into the mind and heart of Alexander as a young man:

> "I saw her heavenly virtues shine so clear
> That I was forced for to conceal my fire,
> And with respects even bridling my desire.
> And though I burned with all the flames of love,
> Yet, frozen with a reverent kind of fears,
> I durst not pour my passions in her ears,
> Lest so I might the hope I have remove."

Not one to give up easily, Alexander makes protestations of his adoring love that reveal the depth and nature of his affection in the hope that she responds in kind:

> "I swear Aurora, by thy starry eyes,
> And by those golden locks whose lock none slips,
> And by the coral of thy rosy lips,
> And by the naked snows which beauty dyes;
> I swear by all the jewels of thy mind,
> Whose like yet never worldly treasure bought,
> Thy solid judgment and thy generous thought,
> Which in this darkened age have clearly shined;
> I swear by those and by my spotless love,
> And by my sacred and most fervent fires,
> That I have never nursed but chaste desires,
> And such as modesty might well approve.
> Then since I love those virtuous parts in thee,
> Should thou not love this virtuous mind in me?"

Failing to get the hoped-for response, the dejected lover-poet laments the loss of the mutual bliss that both could have, if only she would put aside her pride and warm to his love:

> "O, if thou knewest how thou thyself dost harm,
> And dost prejudge thy bliss and spoil my rest,
> Then thou wouldst melt the ice out of thy breast,
> And thy relenting heart would kindly warm.
> O, if thy pride did not our joys control,

What world of loving wonders shouldst thou see!
For if I saw thee once transformed in me,
Then in thy bosom I would pour my soul !"

Resigned to his fate, the poet leaves for foreign lands in the hope of forgetting about her. However, he did not seem to get much relief. These lines indicate Alexander's growing philosophical insight into the intricacies of the human heart, and the depths of human nature:

"Oft have I heard, which now I must deny,
That naught can last it that it be extreme;
Times daily change, and we likewise in them;
Things out of sight do straight forgotten die.
There is nothing more vehement than love,
And yet I burn, and burn still with one flame;
Times oft have changed, yet I remain the same;
Nought from my mind her image can remove.
The greatness of my love aspires to ruth;
Time vows to crown my constancy in th' end,
And absence doth my fancies but extend.
Thus I perceive the poet spoke the truth,
That who to see strange countries were inclined
Might change the air but never change the mind."

In bidding a poetic farewell to the woman who had been the object of his early affections, he hints, with Shakespearean insight, at the possibility that release from his enthralment will enable him to find a more mature and fulfilling love:

"Then farewell crossing joys and joyful crosses!
Most bitter sweets, and yet most sugared sours!
Most hurtful gains, yet most commodious losses,
That made my years to flee away like hours,
And spent the springtime of mine age in vain,
Which now my summer must redeem again."

He assures his *amour* one last time of the immortality of his love with lines that any woman of the time must surely have felt flattered to receive:

"Some yet not born surveying lines of mine,
Shall envie with a sigh, the eyes that view'd
Those beauties which my bloud so oft imbrude,
Then shall they fame ore all untainted flie,
Thou in my lines, and I shall live in thee."

Happily for the love-lorn Alexander, soon after his return to Scotland from abroad, he successfully wooed the young, musically talented, and aristocratic Janet Erskine, whose family had been keepers of Stirling Castle and protectors of princes of the realm. They were married in 1601 and as far as is known their relationship was a happy and fruitful one. She mothered seven sons and three daughters, and outlived him after 40 years of married life.

Alexander's pen was not solely occupied with sonneteering. Although he composed poems in celebration of King James VI's assent to the English throne, he was already tackling more weighty matters and modes of literary expression. He had turned his hand to playwriting.

His education, travels abroad, and awareness of the streams of artistic thought and feeling that were flowing from the south led him to imitate, in theme and structure, the classical playwrights of the past, particularly the Roman, Seneca. A humanist in the inhumane world of Nero's Rome and suspected at times of being sympathetic to the Christian sect, Seneca was influenced by classical Greek dramatists such as Sophicles and Euripides, who posed the philosophical idea that through atonement the disturbed equilibrium of the moral world is rectified and the disturber purified. This was very much in line with the central Renaissance theme of human ennoblement and perfectibility, which also drew its inspiration from sources as diverse as the great Biblical tales and the romances of Ovid. So it was quite natural that in Italy, the country that gave birth to the Renaissance, there had been a return to the classical writers of the past and, by the beginning of the sixteenth century, Senecan tragedy was very much in vogue. It is an interesting observation on the changing educational scene at the time that Seneca's writings were taught by Erasmus and in the Italian humanist schools. This theatrical trend had moved to France by the middle of the century and then went across the channel to England. Queen Elizabeth gave the new style social respectability with a royal command performance, and patronage for English imitators followed.

Such well-known English theatrical figures of the late-sixteenth century as Thomas Kyd and Fulke Greville wrote adaptations or imitations of Seneca's original plays. Never one to ignore a good plot if it was available, even Shakespeare got in on the act. The Senecan school of dramatists was occupied with themes drawn from classical history and their plays were heavy on political philosophy, dealing with such issues as the folly of the pursuit of power and wealth. Such dramatists tried to bring about a rebirth of the Roman political ideal, a more moral political order based on honesty and integrity in high places. These were issues that gave rise to some of Shakespeare's greatest plays, and they spoke strongly to the dramatist Alexander. His first published play appeared in 1603, the year James VI of Scotland moved south to become James I of England. Entitled *The Tragedy of Darius*, the highly stylized drama told the tale of the Persian king and dealt with the trials and tribulations of kings in general, who, once supreme and powerful, when facing death must also face the fact that they too are but human. The play offered much in the way of advice to those in power:

"Of all the passions which possesse the soule,
None so disturbes vaine Mortals mindes,
As vaine Ambition which so blindes
The light of them, that nothing can controll
Nor curb their thoughts who will aspire."

The work was dedicated to James and sweetened with compliments to him, as might be expected from an up-and-coming author in such a society.

Following his appointment as tutor to the young Prince Henry, Alexander wrote a tract entitled *A Paraenesis to the Prince*. An extraordinary work, it is a poem of 84 verses describing the evolution of different civilizations and some of the wiser rulers of earlier times. Intended to instruct the young heir to the throne in the wisdom of the past, it drew heavily on the philosophy of Plato and teachings of other ancients. In lines that hint at his apparent early familiarity with Masonic and Rosicrucian thought, which drank from some of the the the same classical sources, he says:

"Be not those miserable soules,
Their judgements to refine who never strive!

Nor will not looke upon the lerned scroules,
Which without practice do experience give."

Full of audacious admonitions to the future king, it also includes
a warning that misbehaving and unschooled princes who ignore the
lessons of history can be dethroned. Pointing to the moral demise of
past monarchies, he wrote, as if prophetically foreseeing the predica-
ment into which future royals would fall:

"And in all ages it was ever seene
What virtue rais'd, by vice had ruin'd been."

Alexander encouraged his princely pupil to rise above the material temptations of court, learn to discern between the flatterer and
the faithful courtier, and grow in goodness and generosity. Ending
on an optimistic note, he reassured the king-to-be that, with right
living and wise counsel, he would rule a land renowned for its moral
and intellectual strength and the health and prosperity of its people.
Unfortunately, Prince Henry didn't live long enough to apply such
profound advice or to fulfill such a dream in the land he hoped to
one day rule. He died in November 1612, apparently of pneumonia.

In 1604, one year after Henri IV of France gave his blessing to
a band of Frenchmen that included Samuel de Champlain to set up
a French colony in Acadie, Alexander published another Greek-style
poetic drama. Entitled *Croesus*, it introduced the Athenian priest-phi-
losopher Solon to the stage. Again the theme dealt with the tragedy
that befalls those who put their faith in vain ambition, the pursuit of
power, and the banal accumulation of material wealth. The play pays
homage to the insightful and prophetic power of dreams and the
undying power of love that can reach even beyond the grave.
Through several interconnected plots, the avarice and bloated pride
of the king are contrasted with the simple teachings of the philosopher. Similiar to some of Shakespeare's historic dramas, though not
approaching their dramatic brilliance, *Croesus* also had much in the
way of profound advice to offer monarchs of the time.

Alexander also tackled the rise and fall of the empire of his
famous namesake Alexander the Great. In 1605, he published *The
Alexandrean*. A play about Julius Caesar followed in 1607, which
one source states may have provided Shakespeare with lines of dialogue for his play about the Roman Emperor. Along with the earlier

plays, these two formed his highly regarded body of dramatic work known as *The Monarchick Tragedies*. As was the case with the works of the Senecans in France, their didactic style and weighty contents made them more suitable to being read than performed, and this may have been Alexander's intention.

By 1612 Alexander was embarking on commercial and state matters in addition to his responsibilities as Gentleman to the Privy Chamber of Prince Henry, but he still found time to launch into the early stages of his longest poetic composition, which ran to over 11,000 lines. Entitled *Dooms-day* or *The Great Day of The Lord's Judgment*, it is a Biblical epic that extends from the Creation to a treatment of the Book of Revelation. Promising salvation through the redeeming power of Divine Love, it is one of two great religious works Alexander tackled, the other being a metrical translation of the Psalms of David that he began as a collaborative effort with King James. Like other writers of the age, Alexander envisioned a New Jerusalem for which he felt all mankind should tirelessly work. His translation of the Psalms, published after the death of King James, so shocked the Presbyterian clergy of Scotland by its secular language that Alexander was looked upon as both a heathen and a traitor, of which we will hear more later.

By 1616, with his published addition to the unfinished portion of the dead Sir Philip Sidney's acclaimed masterpiece, *Arcadia*, Alexander's literary work had achieved considerable recognition in England, if not in his native Scotland. The completion of *Arcadia* was a major achievement in itself, as it was considered one of the great literary accomplishments of the Elizabethan Renaissance. It also suggests that Alexander had some association with that esoteric group of *literati* who had assembled around the English poet-warrior. Whether *Arcadia*, set as it was in a mythical pastoral kingdom, turned his mind to considering the possibility of one day sending people to settle in territory across the Atlantic is another matter, but it was his interest in doing just that in Nova Scotia that prompted him, in spite of his increasing responsibilities at court, to pick up his pen again after abandoning it for some years. His tract entitled *An Encouragement to Colonies* was published just a few years after he received his Nova Scotia land charter from the King in 1621. Finding himself in heavy debt after giving much of his own personal fortune, and a good deal of his time and attention, to two earlier failed attempts to establish a settlement in Nova Scotia, he now resorted to his pen to arouse some of his fellow countrymen to join him in his historic enterprise. Following in the footsteps of Sir Walter Raleigh, whose earlier publication *The Discovery of Guiana* had aroused much interest in the new world, Alexander hoped his words would awaken some of his fellow countrymen to what he saw as both the opportunity and responsibility that awaited in Nova Scotia. But, *An Encouragement to Colonies* was no ordinary appeal for financial support or settlers. Alexander went into deep background, chronicling the history of colonization from the early days of the Egyptian and the Jewish races. He appealed to his fellow countrymen's national pride, Christian faith, and sense of adventure:

> "I cannot but be confident that my own countrymen are as fit for such a purpose as any men in the world... Where was ever ambition baited with greater hope than here... that this might be our chief end to begin a new life, serving God more sincerely than before, to whom we may draw more near, by retiring ourselves further from hence."

This document perhaps provides the best insight into what so strongly motivated Alexander, as it did others of the early-seventeenth century, to look to North America as a place where they or their offspring could begin to build the New Jerusalem, far away from the religious upheavals, political uncertainties, and the competitive struggles of life in England and Scotland.

Heavily preoccupied with his offices of state and the challenges of political and religious turmoil in England and Scotland, and struggling to keep his Nova Scotia project alive, Alexander didn't publish again until near the end of his life. Then, tiring of public office, his struggles over Nova Scotia, and perhaps sensing that the end was in sight, he withdrew to his Stirling manor house where he gathered his collected works together, picked up his creative pen one last time for some revisions, and had them published in a volume appropriately titled *Recreations with the Muses*.

It needs to be emphasized that Alexander's poetry and plays, though they appear somewhat archaic to the modern ear, were in keeping with the literary styles of the time and dealt with themes both international and universal. This is not to say that he didn't care about his native land. As later chapters will show, he was very much concerned about its welfare. But, as happens in all ages, certain cultural influences dominated while others declined. By the end of the sixteenth century, due to the intellectually strict and culturally repressive nature of the Scottish Reformation, the river of national song, full of love and humour and expressed in the native tongue, had almost ceased to flow. Apart from the *Essayes* of James VI and a few other contributions, Scottish poetry was almost non-existent. With James' ascension to the English throne and the transfer of the court to London in 1603, the ancient Scottish tongue became even more rarely used as a vehicle for literary expression. This was a time when English poetry, prose, and drama were flourishing and England was home to a galaxy of dramatic poets whose likes the world had never seen before, and so it had become almost essential for the literate to read and write in either Latin or English.

Alexander's scholarly education and tastes led him to see the great superiority of English to his native tongue. It was only natural that an emerging Scottish poet, closely connected to the English court and living in London, would express himself in the language of his successful English contemporaries. Fortunately, education and opportunity allowed him to converse and write in both Latin and English with considerable ease and eloquence. Consequently, he became by far the most voluminous Scottish poet of his time writing in the English language, and he encouraged his fellow countrymen to do likewise, saying its was to be preferred for its "elegance and perfection." Naturally, this was resented by many of his fellow Scotsmen and it prevented him from becoming the popular national poet he might otherwise have been.

There is a view that Shakespeare read some of Alexander's work and gained snippets of dialogue, if not a plot or two, by way of the Scot. For instance, in his first play, *Darius*, Alexander presages Shakespeare's much-quoted line, "Uneasy is the head that wears the crown" with his own, "A golden crown doth cover leaden cares."

Of course, this and other examples might be mere coincidences but, as Alexander was resident in London and active at court and in literary circles during Shakespeare's lifetime, it is quite possible that some communication and gentlemanly exchange of ideas took place between the two. That they served the same cause as dramatists and at times drew from the same sources, there can be no doubt. Respected in English literary circles and at court, Alexander was a leading proponent of the establishment of an academy, a place where history, the arts, and the sciences could be studied and recorded. It would be some years after his death before this dream, also shared by such notables as Sir Francis Bacon, became a reality in the form of the Royal Society.

Quickly eclipsed by more brilliant and popular literary lights of his day in England and ignored at home for political and religious reasons, Alexander's poetry, plays, and prose provide us with an insight into the heart and mind of the man of whom his better-remembered fellow poet and friend, William Drummond, wrote, "This Isle too little for his brave muse. A new world must heare his layes." That new world was to be Nova Scotia.

7

Courtier And Statesman

Sir William Alexander

James VI of Scotland's triumphant and peaceful entry onto the English scene in 1603 was a most curious but providential twist of political fate for both countries, especially in view of the long history of animosity and aggression that had existed between the two and the more recent execution of his mother, Mary, by the forces of Elizabeth I. But he was next in line to the throne of England and he had demonstrated his ability to rule well and wisely in Scotland, and most of the English were pleased to have a man on the throne again after living through the long shadow of their complex, though much-beloved Queen. Although James did not cut a handsome or majestic figure and was more an intellectual than a man of action, he already had several publications to his credit, and it seemed appropriate that England should have a learned and literary ruler on the throne. Most importantly, he was committed to peace, and, after the years of unsettling and costly war with Spain, such an attitude was welcome.

The English court was vastly larger and more complex than that which James had known in Scotland, but his appointment of experienced Englishmen to key advisory and administrative positions made the transition to the more powerful throne a lot less troublesome than it might otherwise have been. Of course, a large Scottish retinue accompanied James to London, while others, still occupied with official business at home, soon followed. Among them was William Alexander.

The life of the English court in the wake of Elizabeth's death was one of conscious elegance and purchased grandeur, in spite of the dire financial state of the nation. Elaborate entertainments and lavish state banquets set the social style for much of James' reign. Within the hierarchy of court life, the position and wealth of the ambitious depended very much on royal favour, which more often than not was leveraged by gifts, flattery, and influential friends. But, ability and talent were not ignored, especially if they could be made to serve the King.

It was in such august and alluring surroundings that doors opened for Alexander which led him to high state office and a much improved social and financial status. They also, however, eventually led him away from his pen.

Here Alexander saw for the first time many of the remaining significant men and women of the Elizabethan world, heard of important matters pertaining to the rule of the new realm, witnessed the comings and goings of ambassadors, and shared the excitement surrounding England's success in Atlantic exploration, which had just seen a settlement established by a London-based merchant company at a spot called Jamestown in Virginia.

In 1607, the King granted Alexander the right to mine minerals and metal of all types in his home barony of Menstrie, with a tenth of the proceeds to go to the royal coffers. We can assume from this, and from his earlier written comments, that Alexander had some prior knowledge or experience of mining. The project seems to have proved lucrative, because Alexander applied for and received in 1611 an additional royal grant to set up a silver refinery in the area. It authorized him "to fynne silver with quicksilver, water and salt for twentie ane yeires, secluding all uthers during that space except the Kingis workis."

The experience and profits gained from these operations encouraged Alexander to look further afield for precious metals and, some years later, what seemed like an even more promising opportunity came his way. The King bestowed on him the authority to mine gold and silver, on a much larger scale than he had done at Menstrie, at Crawford Muir in Lanarkshire and at Hilderston in Linlithgowshire. The mines had been successfully worked for several years by the King's own metallurgist, Sir Bevis Bulmer, but, having begun to prove difficult and expensive to work, they were given over to private enterprise. Alexander's enthusiastic involvement in this operation, in which he was joined by Edinburgh goldsmith Thomas Foullis and a Portuguese mining engineer, was apparently based on his belief that, by using cheaper methods of refining the ore at source (something he had learned about at Menstrie) a good return on investment could be made. But the operation turned out to be financially disastrous, as the economic drain caused by the mine's poor return was compounded by a land dispute with one James Ross who, in retaliation for what he considered encroachment on his property, secretly sabotaged the mine. There was also a rash of thefts of ore and equipment by some of the local workers, and by 1614 the writing was on the wall. This was the first of a number of serious financial setbacks for a man who, by temperament and inclination, was probably not well-suited for such hard-headed business enterprises. However, in an age when the entrepreneurial spirit was breaking out all over and new opportunities for accruing private wealth were opening up, one can hardly blame a poet, especially one with a growing family to maintain, for trying his hand at the game. (This early involvement in mining and his association with mining engineers of the time give rise to suspicions that Alexander may have been connected in some way with the creation of the mine-like underground workings on Nova Scotia's mysterious Oak Island, or with early mining operations along the nearby Gold River, of which more later.)

During the early days of his mining operations Alexander and a cousin undertook the demanding task of collecting back taxes, of which they were to receive half, owed to the English Crown for most of the previous 50 years by some of his fellow Scotsmen. This generated little personal return, as might be expected under the circumstances, and, given the historical hatred of tax collectors, the innate animosity of Scotsmen towards the English, and their more impoverished state, this unpopular piece of service quite naturally blackened his name in the minds of many of his fellow countrymen.

Despite these setbacks, Alexander became firmly established as Gentleman of the Privy Chamber, was well connected to the throne through his marriage into the Erskine family, and had a growing reputation as a philosophical man of letters. Indeed, he had become one of the most prominent Scotsman at the English court, so it wasn't surprising that, around 1608, he was knighted by an appreciative King. This was a remarkable accomplishment, especially in view of the fact that many knighthoods of the day were bestowed only on those who either excelled in service to the Crown or could afford to purchase the honour. This latter method quickly becoming the preference of the free-spending King.

Immediately following the unfortunate accidental death of the King's eldest son Henry in 1612, an event that genuinely saddened many in England and prompted Sir William to compose a lament entitled *An Elegy on the Death of Prince Henry*, he was appointed aide and tutor to Henry's younger brother, Prince Charles. So began a relationship that was to last from the physically handicapped Prince's awkward and painful youth, through their entwined fortunes involving Nova Scotia, and into the final tragic years of both their lives.

Having demonstrated his ability to deal with his fellow countrymen, Alexander was appointed in 1615 to the influential and potentially lucrative but challenging office of Master of Requests for Scotland. James I, an astute and crafty assessor of men, determined that Sir William had the ability to deal diplomatically and firmly with problems in Scotland. But, unfortunately for Alexander, he again found himself in the unenviable position of appearing to advance himself at the expense of some of his fellow Scotsmen. In his new position, he was required to act as arbitrator among the ever-increasing number of Scotsmen flocking to London in the hope of receiving either favours or redress from the King. As well as putting him in the role of go-between and lobbyist for some legitimate and influential cases, the position had a harsher aspect. An edict published in relation to the appointment also stated:

> "Sir William Alexander, knyght, Master of Requests for our Kingdome of Scotland has received a commission to apprehend and send home, or to punish all those idle and vagrant persones who come from thence, by their misbehaviour do both trouble us discredite to their country."

Even if he had been a hugely populist poet in his native Scotland, Alexander would have been hard-pressed to overcome the stigma resulting from this latest royal appointment. Nonetheless, he apparently carried out the functions of his new office with diligence, and the King obviously appreciated Alexander's ability to do so. In 1614, he appointed him to the prestigious Scottish Privy Council, the highest advisory body on Scottish affairs short of Parliament, the Scottish Privy Council, which was made up of knowledgeable and influential men whose duty it was to publish and enforce the King's decrees. Such a responsibility placed him at the centre of affairs of state.

An indication of Alexander's objective and compassionate nature was evident in his work as member of the Perth Assembly, a government body that questioned individuals suspected of sedition or treason, usually punishable by death.

Royal forces had moved, quite brutally at times, to suppress the more independent chiefs in western Scotland. As well, James' ecclesiastical policies were reprehensible to the reformed Scottish church, and consequently he was no longer readily seen as the protector of Scottish cultural, political, and religious interests. Opposition voices were raised and many were brought to trial. In June, 1619 an Edinburgh printer was summoned to appear before the Assembly on charges of having published material highly critical of the King's policies. After examining the accused, Alexander, to his credit, proposed that the printer be released, a view unfortunately not shared by others on the panel. On another occasion, Alexander was responsible for restoring an accused member of the Scottish clergy who had been relieved from his duties and his livelihood by the King's commissioners to his former position. It seems that Alexander was capable of rising above the narrow religious sectarianism of the times and of bringing a degree of independent thought, action, and human decency to this demanding work.

His attachment to Glasgow University was demonstrated at this time by his determination to gain for it a fellow Scot's bursary request that had found its way into the pocket of one of the peers of the realm. Using his influence at court and his substantial persuasive powers, Alexander succeeded in establishing the right of the university to the legacy that the deceased benefactor had intended. In appreciation, the university established the Stirling Bursary, which was awarded annually until at least the time of Alexander's death.

Both Alexander's literary ability and his growing knowledge of state affairs qualified him in 1621 to become one of the Lords of the Articles, whose special business it was to prepare bills for submission to Parliament. By such timely appointments of capable and dedicated men, James was able to govern still-unruly Scotland from a distance, enabling him to boast to the amazed and amused members of the English Parliament that, "Here I sit and govern it with my pen, I write and it is doneà which others could not do with the sword."

James was now head of the Anglican Church and was opposed by the Scottish reformers. Alexander, because of his frequent trips to Edinburgh and his knowledge of the volatile political and religious situation in Scotland, had served as a diplomatic letter carrier, and this likely cast him into the role of secret service agent to the Crown. Perhaps because he had travelled abroad and did not belong to any of the camps of religious extremists, he was also called into service as a secret peace negotiator between the Vatican and the British Crown. Equally important in his being chosen for such a task may have been the fact that he was a recognized man of learning and his universal spiritual outlook was a matter of public record. There is also the possibility that the Masonic Order, which even then embraced men of many faiths, may have played a role in his selection, since it seems certain that the King, and possibly Alexander, were members of this fraternity that had sympathisers in every country on the continent, and even within the Church of Rome.

On ascending to the English throne, James made it known that his desire internationally was to create peace among his own and other nations. He expressed an interest in resurrecting the former Christian Empire of Europe by bringing together the various warring factions that had long been at each other's throats. This was James' abiding desire, to be unifier and peacemaker. At home, he wisely stayed the religious course charted by his predecessor Elizabeth. Anglicanism remained the state-sanctioned faith, but now with a new degree of toleration for both the wary Catholics and the constantly complaining English reformers, the Puritans. However, fears and suspicions lingered, and neither the Catholics nor the Puritans responded wholeheartedly to James' overtures. With or without the help of Jesuit accomplices, a band of fanatical Catholics determined that it would be best for both their religion and their country if they were to blow up Parliament, with the King and his family inside. Following the failed and now farcical Gunpowder Plot, which involved the legendary Guy Fawkes, Catholics in England were under serious suspicion. The threat that the King might be assassinated remained, as it was known that some Jesuits had preached that regicide was a redeemable offence. Elizabeth's anti-Catholic laws were re-enacted, and all persons failing to toe the Anglican line were heavily fined. A few Catholic rebels were executed, some were imprisoned, and others had their lands and holdings confiscated. Inevitably, both Puritans in England and Presbyterians in Scotland opposed the monarch's role in church matters and threatened further civil unrest, if not open rebellion. In the early 1620s, Pope Gregory XV let it be known that James could count on the loyalty of English Catholics, as long as they were treated with the respect due fellow believers. Alexander was brought into the subsequent secret correspondence, meetings, and discussions, handling letters between the King and the papal nuncio in Brussels. He also participated in important negotiations with a papal representative sent secretly to England in the hope of peacefully regaining lands previously ruled by James' son-in-law, Friederich of the Palatinate, husband of James' daughter Elizabeth, whose court at Heidelberg had become one of the esoteric and mystical learning centres of Europe. Friederich's acceptance of the vacant throne of Bohemia, seen by Catholics as a step toward spreading his particular politico-religious outlook in the rest of Europe, led to the outbreak of prolonged hostilities, and to Friederich and Elizabeth's exile into Holland. It seems the Vatican was seeking a diplomatic solution to the German land issue, and so it held out the carrot of Catholic compliance with James' Anglican rule.

In 1624, Alexander was sent on a highly secret mission to Rome where he discussed, among other matters, the Oath of Allegiance required of all James' subjects and the possibility of a marriage between the King's second son, Charles, and the Catholic princess, Henrietta Maria of France. A papal dispensation was needed for the young princess in order for the marriage to proceed, and Alexander was considered to be the King's most suitable advocate. The fact that he was believed to be a secret Catholic by some in diplomatic circles on the continent and at home was, under the circumstances, also an asset.

While in Florence, Sir William came down with such a life-threatening sickness that Cardinal Francesco Barberini, a nephew of the Pope, received word that Alexander would likely die. Given the deep-rooted and widespread opposition to any such match back in England and Scotland, this was certainly a dangerous mission, and it is possible that some foul play was involved. However, providence intervened and Alexander recovered. The dispensation was granted, Maria Henrietta's personal religious rights were guaranteed, and a generous dowry was agreed upon. The marriage took place in 1625, and it was to have future implications, not only for Charles and England, but also for Alexander and the dream to which he was to devote most of his fortune, time, and talents for the rest of his life.

Alexander's status, close connections at court, and involvement in state affairs acquainted him with efforts already underway by men from France and England to establish permanent trading and religious settlements in the wilderness of the North American continent. Jamestown was firmly established, Québec was growing, the Massachusetts Bay colony was on its way, and some hardy souls had even managed to settle in Newfoundland. A few years prior to the death in 1625 of King James I, Alexander began to seek an opportunity to play a personal and patriotic part in this colonization of the new world, to add his own efforts to such exciting and adventurous developments. As yet undiscovered riches and resources might bring fame and fortune to Alexander, his King, and his country. In Alexander's fertile mind, it was becoming ever more obvious that a heroic opportunity awaited him, one by which he might address the pressing needs and alleviate the hardships of many struggling to survive in his native Scotland. Since there already existed a New France and a New England, why not also a New Scotland? In his fellow countryman the King, Sir William found an enthusiastic supporter for such an enterprise.

8

Atlantic Adventurers

Alexander's dream of settlement in the new world, and his son William's eventual success at Charlesfort in southwest Nova Scotia, came after more than a century and a half of trans-Atlantic adventuring by others.

The lure of lands on the other side of the wide Atlantic pre-dates by many years the well-documented 1492 voyage of navigator and explorer Christopher Columbus. Prior to his attempt to find a westerly sea route to the Land of the Great Khan on behalf of the Spanish monarchy, the experienced and expert Italian seaman, a man who diligently studied books on geography, history, travel, cosmography, and natural history, is known to have put some stock in fables and fishermen's tales that told of lands far out in the ocean to the west. The European Renaissance, with its renewed interest in ancient literature and its translation of Greek texts, had brought to light Plato's references to Atlantis, which the Egyptians believed had existed far out in the Atlantic. A document written by the Greek historian Diodorus in the first century B.C. told of an island far out in the Atlantic, off the coast of Africa, that had been discovered by the Phoenicians. The *Annals* of the sixth-century Irish monk St. Brendan described the fantastic adventures he and a number of his clerical brethren experienced while voyaging westwards to reach the Isle of the Blessed. Viking sagas told of the exploits of Leif Erickson and other Norsemen who found and explored bountiful lands southwest of Greenland around 1000 A.D.

One of the consequences of the Crusades of the Middle Ages, which brought the Knights Templars to the Middle East, was that nautical and cartographic knowledge long the preserve of the Arab and Muslim world was brought back to Europe. Such knowledge is believed to have led Prince Henry the Navigator of Portugal, Grand Master of the Templars, now re-named the Knights of Christ, to establish his renowned school of navigation. Its graduates reached

Madeira and the Azores, and sailed down the west coast of Africa with the original, eight-pointed, red Templar cross emblazoned on their sails.

During the latter part of the fifteenth century and the early part of the sixteenth, a number of European sailors ventured into the waters of the Atlantic to explore the great divide between the coastlines of their native lands and the unknown regions beyond the western horizon. Some 70 years before Columbus set sail, the Portuguese, known even then to have sailed as far as Greenland and Labrador, had mapped islands in the western Atlantic, one of which they named Antilia.

While there was a growing preoccupation with finding a westerly route to the riches of China and India, some held out the possibility of finding exotic lands of legend and lore, such as the pastoral paradise of Arcadia, the Land of Seven Cities, St. Brendan's Isle, Hy Brazil or Tir na N'Og, the Land of Youth of Celtic mythology. In fact, one of Columbus' associates, Ponce de Leon, scouted the islands of the Bahamas as far as the Florida coast in search of the latter. Regardless of what he personally thought of such matters, there is no doubt that Columbus' profound faith gave his quest an almost mystical facet. He felt chosen by God and saw signs of divine providence in favourable winds, currents, phenomena at sea, and his initial contact with friendly island natives. With the sails of his three ships openly displaying the Templar cross, it was hardly surprising that he named his island landfall in the Bahamas San Salvador (Holy Saviour). Although he died believing he had found a westerly route to the Far East, others in Europe realized that he had really stumbled upon a vast intervening continent, a new world full of exciting possibilities and unknown riches.

In the years following Columbus' 1492 voyage, the militant Spanish expanded their colonial empire on the Central American mainland, mining the territory for everything they could get. The Portuguese were quick to follow, and soon the two monarchies were disputing each other's claim to the whole continent. It took a papal decision in 1493 to resolve the dispute, in which the Spanish Pope favoured his native country while Portugal settled for Brazil.

John Cabot, whose real name was Giovanni Gaboto and who was Italian by birth, sailing across the Atlantic in 1497 in the service of King Henry VII of England, was also hoping to reach Asia. He came upon Newfoundland or Nova Scoia instead, and then sailed farther south. Although he was probably not the first man sailing from England to get there, Cabot's arrival in the new world gave the English a more legitimate claim, in the feudal, political sense, to North America than any the Spanish could muster. In 1500, the Corte-Real brothers, sailing out of the Azores on behalf of King Emmanuel of Portugal, found their way to Newfoundland and Labrador. Joam Fagundes, another Portuguese, followed twenty years later. Not to be out-manoeuvred, the French under Francis I got into the act with a free-wheeling Italian navigator by the name of Giovanni Verrazzano. But, unlike the Spanish in Central America, none of these nations, although they all laid claim to the North American continent, made any early serious efforts to colonize it.

Asserting that King Arthur had sent a group of Scots on an even earlier English voyage to this continent 1,000 years previously, John Dee, astrologer and quasi-navigational historian to Elizabeth I, encouraged her to consider herself Queen of a trans-Atlantic empire. In 1536, there surfaced a Venetian claim that they had been among the first Europeans to reach North America. Historian Marco Barbaro published his *Discendenza Patrizie*, a biographical dictionary of Venetian notables in which he mentioned that, late in the fourteenth century, the Venetian navigator Antonio Zeno, a member of a well-known seafaring family, had accompanied the prince of a northern land across the Atlantic to a new continent. The accompanying map of the North Atlantic depicted a surprisingly accurate coastline of Greenland and what appears to be the northeast coast of Newfoundland. The Zeno map was used by several later explorers. Some researchers have concluded that the prince in question was likely the fourteenth-century Earl of the Orkneys, Prince Henry Sinclair.

Meanwhile English seamen out of Bristol were gaining experience of northern waters because of their active trade with Iceland. The growing demand for fish and fish oil, and the profit to be gained from both, pushed them even farther west. Driven from the Icelandic coastline by Danish interests, English fishermen then ventured into waters where, according to one source, the cod fish were so plentiful "that a boat could hardly be rowed through them." Between the middle and end of the sixteenth century, the seas off Newfoundland and Nova Scotia were lucrative fishing grounds frequented by British, French, Portuguese, and Spanish vessels. Sir Francis Bacon, who had an appreciative knowledge of the riches of the natural world and was connected to at least two of the early English settlements in

North America, declared of the Grand Banks, "They contain richer treasures than the mines of Mexico and Peru." History was to prove him right.

The general practice among those who made up these fishing fleets was to build temporary drying or oiling stations along the coast. The work of the fishing season finished, these would then be abandoned until next year. As might be expected, the competitive nature of this seasonal fishery led to conflict among the various nations engaged in it and sometimes involved races or stand-offs to hold onto stations from year to year. Equipment and structures left behind sometimes went missing, or were destroyed by natives, pirates, or privateers. A sixteenth-century version of later fishing wars developed.

This situation made it important to establish at least temporary shoreline settlements in order to hold ground, protect equipment and structures left behind, and provide some advantage to vessels arriving in the spring. There was even talk of establishing permanent shoreline outposts. Anthony Parkhurst, an enterprising English fish merchant, whose interests were as much pecuniary as patriotic, is known to have visited Newfoundland in 1577 and declared it to be suitable for habitation by Englishmen. None seemed too eager, however, to act on his pronouncement.

Along with these fishing interests, England's growing naval prowess and her continuing desire to be first to find a northwest passage to China encouraged its seamen to strike out across the Atlantic. The age bred a number of courageous and determined sailors such as Martin Frobisher, John Davis, and Henry Hudson, whose names and accomplishments are now part of Canadian history and geography. There were also free-booting patriotic privateers such as John Hawkins, who ventured southwest into the Spanish-held Caribbean in search of gold and glory. In Hawkins' wake came Francis Drake, who circumnavigated the globe, daringly and profitably raiding Spanish ships and ports en route.

By the late-sixteenth century, the Atlantic had become a highway to heroic and profitable adventures and the coastline of the still little-explored continent was a place where romantic dreams coloured by myth and legend could be realized by men willing and capable of taking the main chance. Since the Spanish had been fortunate in finding gold and other wealth to the south, might not the same be possible in the cooler and still-unsettled regions to the north?

And if not precious metals or stones, there was always the abundance of fish, furs, and skins by which one could turn a profit. But fame and honours still awaited the man who could find an opening to the East, and the fabulous lands of legend might yet be found. Consequently, two of the most characteristic English figures of the era spanning the reigns of Elizabeth I and James I were the ambitious, usually well-educated, gentleman adventurer and the risk-taking maritime merchant who participated in trans-Atlantic enterprises. Some of these men shared Dee's enthusiasm for the expansion of English interests in North America, and also nurtured dreams of finding another Avalon or Arcadia.

One such individual was the entrepreneurial aristocrat Sir Humphrey Gilbert who, after selling off half his estates and fitting out five ships, sailed from Plymouth to St. John's, Newfoundland in 1583. Upon his arrival and on the basis of John Cabot's voyage of nearly a century before, he arbitrarily reclaimed it on behalf of his Queen and country. Sailing south, he lost his supply ship and many of his men on the shoals of Sable Island and then abandoned plans to reach the coast of what was then known as Norumbega, later called New England. During his return to England, his own tiny, eight-ton frigate, the *Squirrel*, sank in high seas. According to a fellow adventurer, the spirited Gilbert, realizing his fate, began reading Sir Thomas Moore's *Utopia* on deck and called out to his fearful companions, "We are as near to heaven by sea as by land" as his ship went down.

This dramatic tale of Gilbert's loss at sea, far from deterring others from taking up the challenge, achieved what was perhaps its intended purpose, that of strengthening their resolve. Plans were suggested for permanent settlement as a means of controlling the fishery in northeastern waters but were not acted upon because of wars involving France and Spain, and it was to be some years later before Englishmen would try to settle the New Found Land. With additional information about the coastal geography and climatic conditions gained from French sources, at least one English exploratory vessel in the late 1590s skirted the eastern coast of Nova Scotia, where it was felt conditions would be more suitable for an English settlement than in Newfoundland.

The Spanish, having established themselves in much of Central America, reached up into present-day Florida, where they quickly dispatched a few courageous Frenchmen. Growing national pride, naval prowess, and profits from English privateering exploits in the Caribbean had given men such as Sir Walter Raleigh added incentive to try to establish an English base north of the Spanish-held lands. Glowing reports brought back to England by members of Raleigh's first exploratory expedition in 1584 impressed the likes of the wealthy poet-adventurer Sir Philip Sidney and the powerful Secretary of State, Sir Francis Walsingham. They contributed to voyages in 1585 and 1587, which both landed settlers on Roanoke, off the coast of present-day North Carolina. The first group of Roanoke Island settlers, concerned for their survival, decided to return to England when given the option to do so by Francis Drake, who stopped by on his way home from one of his sallies into Spanish waters to the south. Due to war with Spain, the Roanoke colony of 1587 could not be re-supplied for two years. When help finally did arrive, the settlers were nowhere in sight. In spite of the best efforts of explorer John Smith, the colony vanished without a trace and went down in history as early America's "lost colony." Although unsuccessful, Raleigh's efforts to establish an English foothold on the North American mainland raised public awareness in England of such a possibility and paved the way for the later plantation in Virginia. Improved geographical knowledge, ship design, and navigational know-how made it inevitable that others would follow. Sad to say, Raleigh's contribution to new-world adventurism did not save him from a harsh death at home. Neither approving of nor popular with James I, he was found guilty of treasonous behaviour and sent to the Tower of London. Not one to twiddle his thumbs or rant at fate, this erudite and philosophical-minded Elizabethan man of action conducted scientific experiments and wrote extensively during his long imprisonment.

After nearly thirteen years in the Tower, Raleigh bought his release and set sail for Guiana, hoping to find gold along the Orinoco River. Promising under pain of death not to interfere with any Spaniards, with whom James was then maintaining a peace, he arrived at his destination only to find the Spanish barring his progress. In the ensuing fight, the dead included Raleigh's own son. Mutiny and desertion followed, and a disheartened Raleigh returned home to face the King's wrath and, after a failed attempt to escape to France, the executioner's axe.

By 1602 the northeastern coast of present-day New England had been explored by Bartholomew Gosnold, who named such well-known spots as Cape Cod and Martha's Vineyard. A 1605 expedition brought back a glowing account of the plant life and favourable climate of the area. The possibility of Englishmen settling such a place interested a number of enterprising individuals, including Sir Ferdinando Gorges of Plymouth, who was to play a key role in Alexander's decision to create a New Scotland. Economic expansion in Europe caused fishing and fur-trading interests to push farther down the Atlantic coast from Newfoundland, and deeper into the St. Lawrence region, in search of new and richer resources. The English national outlook on trans-Atlantic exploration was given a practical and scientific shot in the arm in the 1590s by the writings of Richard Hakluyt, the meticulous recorder of, and commentator on, exploratory voyages to that time.

Soon after King James I effected a peaceable settlement with the Spanish, the business of trans-Atlantic adventuring arose again at court. A syndicate of London and west-coast entrepreneurs, leading merchants, and members of the aristocracy, which is believed to have included Sir William Alexander, brought a proposal to the King. The company, known as the Virginia Company of London and Plymouth, received its historic charter on April 10, 1606, authorizing it to cross the Atlantic and seek to settle in lands extending from latitudes 34° N to 45°N.

Combining political, commercial, and religious interests, this enterprise was a major advancement on all earlier attempts to put Englishmen and women on the east coast of North America. The venture was divided into two sub-companies. Representing predominantly London interests, the Virginia Company focussed on a landfall in Virginia while the North Virginia Company set its sights on establishing a settlement somewhere farther north. The result was that the three ships, the *Susan Constant*, the *Godspeed*, and the *Discovery*, sailed down the Thames on December 20, 1606 and into Chesapeake Bay on April 26, 1607. After disembarking briefly at Cape Henry on the outskirts of the Bay, the settlers sailed some 60 miles inland and went ashore at a more suitable site, where they built the settlement of Jamestown. After weathering some very difficult early years, its inhabitants succeeded in planting a permanent English settlement in North America. History and a new nation were in the making.

On May 30, 1607 the founding expedition of the Plymouth branch of the company left England. The two ships, carrying roughly

100 settlers, landed in mid-August at a site near the mouth of the Kennebec River in Maine, where they built Fort St. George. After a tough winter, several deaths, and poor trading, the settlement was abandoned.

In 1610 the Dutch joined the trans-Atlantic race with an excursion into the mouth of the Hudson River. A trading post was set up on Manhattan Island in territory the Dutch, following the trend of the times, called New Amsterdam.

Perceiving the national and commercial benefits that could result from an English settlement in more northern waters, a large group of court nobles and officials, banded together as the Newfoundland Company, proposed one. Newfoundland had been claimed at one time or another by every nation that had sent fishing or whaling expeditions into the surrounding waters. However, the Spanish, the Portuguese, and the French had all failed to set up any permanent residence on the island. So, in May, 1610 The Newfoundland Company was granted a charter by King James. A colony at Cuper's Cove in Conception Bay was established under the control of Sir John Guy, who had earlier been interested in New England settlement. This "plantation," which grew some of its own food and raised hens, goats, and pigs, suffered not only from the dreaded scurvy but also from internal political conflict. Guy ran afoul of opposition back home and his settlement attracted the unwanted attention of the notorious and powerful pirate Peter Easton and his fleet. In 1615, Guy returned to England, to be replaced as leader of the plantation by Captain John Mason, who remained for another three years. Soon after returning to England in 1619, Mason published an account of his experience. Entitled *A Brief Discourse of the New-Found-Land*, it attracted the attention of Alexander, who had by then decided to try his own hand at trans-Atlantic adventuring. After an informative and mutually agreeable meeting with Mason at his London residence, Alexander acquired property in Newfoundland northwest of Placentia Bay, where he intended to send settlers. But he never did, because Sir Ferdinando Gorges of Plymouth offered him a much larger and more promising tract of land on the mainland.

The Northern Virginia Company had re-grouped as the Council of New England with Gorges as its Secretary. By 1620, it had granted lands around Massachusetts Bay to a group of Puritan brethren anxious to remove themselves from the religious uncertainties and impurities of England to settle where they could live, and govern themselves, according to their own strict interpretation of the Bible. Other English settlements in North America, although they adhered closely to the state religion and remained loyal to the monarchy, were by now offering settlers freedoms, opportunities, and rights they hadn't enjoyed at home, as a more democratic form of government was slowly evolving in these trans-Atlantic outposts.

Hearing from Gorges that the New England Company was anxious to add other plantations to the north and east of Massachusetts Bay, Alexander, by now sensing that his dream of new-world settlement could be realized in more hospitable territory and on his own terms, approached his friend the King about New Scotland.

Meanwhile, the French had also been active in North America. Their early failure in Florida at the hands of the entrenched Spanish had forced them to look farther to the north for a suitable place to establish their New France. With the encouragement of King Henri IV, they turned once again to the territories earlier explored by Jacques Cartier in the St. Lawrence region. In 1603, Henri's cartographer, Samuel de Champlain, travelled to the trading post of Tadoussac to explore the territory. Previous experience of severe winters and loss of life in the area did not encourage settlement. Champlain wrote about his observations and discoveries, including an account, from a French trader, of Indian tales of copper mines farther south. Then in 1604, with Champlain as navigator, the French nobleman Sieur de Monts and a large party set out from the port of La Havre for territory south of the St. Lawrence. De Monts had been granted a monopoly of trade in the region reaching from latitude 40° N to 46°N, which encompassed the attractive and inviting coastline from Long Island to Cape Breton. De Monts' royal decree referred to him as Lieutenant-General of Acadie.

9

Port Royal in Acadie

Long before King Henri IV of France gave his blessing in 1603 to plans for a fur-trading and mineral exploration settlement in the land referred to as Acadie, French fur traders had established seasonal outposts on the northern shore of the St. Lawrence. French fishermen, along with those of other nations, had for many years been fishing during summer in waters off the coasts of Newfoundland, Cape Breton, and mainland Nova Scotia. The French had also tried to find a northern sea route to the Orient and, although unsuccessful, had learned enough to suggest that permanent settlement was possible on the northeast coast of the continent, far from the powerful Spanish.

Although Columbus died believing he had reached Asia, those who followed him soon realized otherwise. A new continent had been discovered, one that offered riches of its own. The coffers of the Spanish monarchy swelled with an abundance of gold and silver taken from conquered peoples and territories. Military commanders succeeded, in spite of some opposition from within Spain and from outspoken members of the Dominican Order, in brutally establishing themselves in parts of Central and South America as ruthlessly acquisitive masters. Spain's dizzying new wealth and power naturally had other European nations wondering whether they too could benefit from exploring this new world. The Portuguese found a footing in Brazil. The French began to look northward.

The luxury-loving Francis I commissioned Giovanni da Verrazzano to sail to North America to stake a French claim to riches similiar to those flowing into the Spanish court, and he reached the coast of Florida in 1524. Steering his lone ship clear of Spanish clutches, he sailed north up the coast as far as Newfoundland, with stops on the way to note coastline conditions. Passing by present-day Virginia and Maryland and liking what he saw, he named it Arcadia, after the idyllic, pastoral kingdom of Greek legend. In time, other cartographers and explorers, perhaps self-servingly, attached this alluring name to territories farther up the coast. Based on Verrazzano's periodic landings, France laid claim to everything he saw and recorded. Although his glowing account of a veritable paradise waiting to be explored excited much interest back in France, no immediate attempt was made to send out settlers.

Interest still focussed on finding a passage to the riches of the Far East or the mythical Island of the Seven Cities. With such objectives in mind, St. Malo sea captain Jacques Cartier set out into the Atlantic on April 20, 1534. Favoured by the elements, he sailed past Newfoundland some twenty days later and into what he called the Grande Baie. From Cartier's notes comes his grim, Biblical observation that the bleak north shore of this enormous gulf resembled "the land God gave to Cain." Travelling south, he went ashore on the more inviting Gaspé Peninsula, where he planted a huge cross and claimed the entire territory for his King. What a group of local Indians, possibly Mohawks, who had been temporarily pacified with various gifts, thought of the proceedings as they looked on, can only be imagined. Cartier's second voyage of exploration brought him farther up the St. Lawrence. Hoping he had found a watercourse that would lead him all the way to Cathay, he sailed passed Tadoussac and other summer landing places of fishermen and traders as far as the rapids near the Indian settlement of Hochelaga. Realizing now that he was, in fact, in an ever-narrowing river, and with time running out, Cartier and his men prepared to overwinter at a fortified site near the mouth of the St. Charles River. Here, Frenchmen for the first time experienced the fierce onslaught of a Canadian winter. Unprepared for such unrelenting cold, winds, and snow, and lacking an adequate diet, 50 men perished, most due to scurvy. Some relief came their way in the form of a native cure that involved drinking tea made by boiling leaves and bark of white spruce. But there was also native resentment to this European encroachment, and Cartier and his remaining men escaped before a threatened attack. In his report to Henri, Cartier remarked that, although the winter was harsh, the soil was fertile upriver and that mineral riches might exist to the north of this land, known to the Indians as Canada.

Cartier's several well-promoted and publicized voyages to the St. Lawrence region did not result in any hoped-for mineral riches or permanent settlement, in spite of efforts in that direction in 1541 and 1542. These attempts, which involved men and women of both high and low rank, were carried out with more panache than good planning, and were fraught with disease and death. Both failed to survive beyond the first winter. Following earlier setbacks in Florida and Brazil, the French abandoned the idea of colonization and, like the English, occupied themselves with lucrative fishing and fur trading in the northeast and with occasional raids on Spanish treasure ships returning home through more southern waters.

For the next 50 years, France was preoccupied with the torments of internal religious war that left little time or resources for empire-building. However, with the coming of peace in 1598, the subject of North America and Canada was raised again at court, and the industrious and pragmatic Henri of Navarre, now King Henri IV, gave royal assent to a proposal for yet another attempt to establish a trading colony on the far side of the Atlantic. Frenchmen were encouraged to face the challenge and opportunity of Canada once again, to establish a New France in the new world.

First to try his luck was a Breton nobleman, the Marquis de la Roche, whose one attempt at settlement was made by a motley group of former prisoners and a few head of cattle, who were deposited on the shores of isolated and wave-swept Sable Island. It was five years before this bizarre experiment came to an end, when a few scrawny survivors were rescued from their desolate existence on the shifting island of sand. As would befall many others who tried to establish new-world colonies, de la Roche incurred enormous debts, was hounded by his creditors, was imprisoned, and died a pauper. Such were the risks undertaken by many trans-Atlantic adventurers, as Sir William Alexander would himself unfortunately discover.

The reign of Henri IV brought relative peace and prosperity to France and resulted in religious freedom for Huguenots, enabling them to occupy positions of power and gain the support of the King.

In 1599, the Huguenot naval commander Pierre de Chauvin de Tonnetuit, who had supported the new King, was given a charter to establish a fur-trading company in New France, of which he was appointed Lieutenant-General. This charter encompassed all known territory on the northeast seaboard between latitudes 40°and 46°N, along with those unknown regions yet to be explored in the interior. One of his partners in this venture was a wealthy merchant named Pont Grave. They were obliged to finance the voyage and the establishment of a permanent, fortified trading centre at Tadoussac, but they were opposed by some of their own countrymen who had prospered from trade in furs and skins with the native Montagnais and the rich fishing grounds of the St. Lawrence. These people had much to lose by the granting of an exclusive licence to someone else, and there was likely some religious rivalry involved as well. In spite of this opposition and the tragic results of earlier efforts in the region, Chauvin and his associates persisted.

In 1600, they sent a party of men to overwinter at Tadoussac. Among the sixteen men left with supplies, disease, hunger, and death took a heavy toll. A mission to rescue the survivors, some of whom had joined Indian bands, brought the French nobleman Sieur de Monts to the continent for the first time.

On the death of Chauvin, the authority to further explore New France was handed to Aymer de Chaste, Governor of Dieppe and Marshall of the Order of St. John of Jerusalem. De Chaste hired the knowledgeable 35-year-old Samuel de Champlain as observer and cartographer for what was to be an exploratory voyage up the St. Lawrence.

The son of a sea captain from Brouage, Champlain had already crossed the Atlantic to the Caribbean in command of a Spanish vessel, and had written about his observations and experiences in a book titled *Brief Discours*. It was avidly read in France by those whose thoughts were once again turning westward across the Atlantic.

In 1603, undaunted by previous failures, Champlain, Pont Grave, and a number of other Frenchmen sailed up the Great River of Canada, where Champlain got his first glimpse of the towering rockface on which he would later establish Québec, which was to be his home for much of the rest of his life. He spent three weeks carrying out an exacting reconnaissance of the St. Lawrence River region and, in detailed journals which would later be published back in France, he noted that, although the land around Tadoussac was unsuitable for settlement, the area beyond present-day Québec was more promising. He also drew attention to ongoing hostilities among the Algonquin tribes and their avowed enemy, the Iroquois, and recorded rumours passed on by a Captain Prevert of St. Malo about the existence of copper mines farther to the south, in a territory known as Arcadia. Prevert, who had been to Canada the previous year, claimed he had been taken by Indian guides down the coast to a copper mine at the head of a large bay, where a mountain stood glistening in the sun.

Champlain's published account of his journey, filled with geographical notes, charts, descriptions of Indians in the region, and references to mines, were as highly prized back in France as the two shiploads of animal skins that arrived there that fall. Unfortunately for de Chaste, he did not live to savour the success of his first step in his plan to create a lucrative fur-trading monopoly in New France.

On Champlain's next trans-Atlantic voyage, he searched for minerals and discovered a beautiful natural harbour, to which he gave the name Port Royal. Here, 25 years later, Sir William Alexander's settlement of Charlesfort would be established.

In 1604, just as Alexander was publishing his early work and hoping to follow King James south to London, Pierre du Guast, Sieur de Monts, a Huguenot merchant from Saintonge with influence at the French court, succeeded in acquiring de Chaste's charter and a ten-year monopoly of the fur trade in New France. Appointed Lieutenant-General by King Henri IV, the debonair de Monts, who had already been to the St. Lawrence region, decided to try his luck with a settlement in the more inviting terrain southwest of Cape Breton, where it was expected Frenchmen would have a much better chance of survival. Fishermen and traders had spoken of its milder climate, productive soil, and friendly native population, and Champlain had reported there was also a possibility of finding mineral deposits in the region.

The French king obviously approved of the proposal, because de Monts' charter authorized him to explore and settle in Acadie. Supported financially by a few sympathetic associates from such trading ports as La Rochelle and St. Malo, the newly appointed Lieutenant-General of New France set sail with Champlain and fellow French nobleman Jean de Biencourt, Sieur de Poutrincourt, on March 7, 1604. Included in the two-ship expedition was a contingent of over 100 artisans, labourers, soldiers, and convicts, as well as two churchmen, a Catholic and a Protestant, who, arguing repeatedly throughout the voyage westward, carried the bitter religious feud of the past with them across the Atlantic. De Monts hoped to put down permanent roots and become self-sufficient, so there were masons, carpenters, and a metal smith in the party, and the ships carried grain and vegetable seed, agricultural implements, and even some livestock. As was the case with many future settlements in North America, the move to Acadie stemmed in part from a desire to find greater free-

The author at Port Mouton beach.

dom and peace in an entirely new environment as well as to establish a profitable trading centre and gain glory for France.

In early May, the main party reached the south shore of Nova Scotia, where a point of land was sighted and named Cape LaHave. Here, they dropped anchor, and the sea-weary but excited adventurers got their first close-up view of the land that was to be their new home.

Some 60 kilometres farther down the coast, they entered a sandy, sheltered bay, and it was decided to disembark at this inviting spot. But, before they could do so, one of the sheep on the vessel jumped overboard, perhaps excited by the sight and smell of fresh vegetation. The incident, which proved futile to the sheep, gave Port Mouton its unique name. Temporary dwellings were set up and the local rabbit population (and probably the over-anxious sheep as well) provided welcome relief from the ship's monotonous fare.

During the next few weeks, Champlain and a handful of others explored the coastline farther south in the ship's *patache*, a small boat equipped with a manoeuvrable sail. Rounding Cape Sable, they headed northwest past present-day Yarmouth, where they named a point of land Cape Forchu on their way to St. Mary's Bay. They explored the shoreline and numerous islands rich in bird life, filling their larder with the cormorant eggs, gannets, and young seals they found in abundance. Somewhere along the way, on one of their trips ashore in search of ore deposits, the Catholic priest, Fr. D'Aubrey, wandered into the thick woods and was lost. Unable to find him, the others proceeded west and north into the opening to a much larger bay they named Baie Francaise (the Bay of Fundy) which they apparently explored briefly in hope of sighting the sought-after mines. On their return journey, the missing Fr. D'Aubrey was still nowhere in sight and, assuming him lost for good, they returned to Port Mouton in early June where they found their supply ship, which had first sailed to the St. Lawrence, had arrived. The temporary camp was promptly abandoned and the whole party sailed toward the Bay of Fundy.

After anchoring in St. Mary's Bay, they were surprised to see the forlorn figure of Fr. D'Aubrey waving frantically to them from the shoreline. His reappearance finally put to rest rumours that Protestants in the party, tired of his incessant religious arguments, had plotted together to dispose of him.

They found no suitable place for settlement in this area, so Champlain, de Monts, and a few others took the ship's boat on into the Bay of Fundy. Sailing northeast along the coast for about 40 kilometres, they sighted a channel through a narrow opening in the mountainous shoreline. It led into what Champlain described in his journal as "one of the finest harbours I had seen on all these coasts, where a couple of thousand vessels could lie in safety. The entrance

Annapolis Royal today

is eight hundred paces wide, and leads into a port two leagues long and one league wide, which I named Port Royal."

All agreed this area offered good possibilities for settlement, and Poutrincourt in particular was anxious to stay in its idyllic surroundings. However, they returned to the Bay of Fundy in hopes of sighting copper deposits farther along the shoreline. Some 50 kilometres up the coast, they crossed the bay to a point they called the Cape of Two Bays, not far from Advocate Harbour. From here, they sailed into Chignecto Bay, which they also crossed before sailing south again along the coast of New Brunswick, still searching for ore and a defensible location for settlement.

Passing the estuary of a large river on June 24th, they named it the St. Jean, it being the feast day of St. John the Baptist. Farther to the south, where New Brunswick and Maine now meet, they came to a river de Monts named the St. Croix, because two tributaries on either side formed the shape of a cross. Considering this location well-suited to their purpose, they decided to settle on an island upriver. Once the decision was made, there was little time to lose. There were defences to mount, buildings to construct, and land to be cleared and sowed. In November Poutrincourt returned to France for additional supplies. Although the site appeared promising, it turned out to be a disastrous choice. The island's soil was too sandy to produce any decent crops, so they had to rely on what could be grown in plots on the mainland. Once the island's wood supply had been used up, fuel also had to be brought from the mainland. Although the site was farther south than Paris, the winter that year was viciously severe, even to those who had already experienced Canadian winters in the St. Lawrence region. In spite of the experience of Cartier's men over 50 years earlier, little had been learned about the nutritional requirements of such settlements. The diet of salt meat and legumes and the severe cold had inevitable results. The dreaded scurvy struck hard and knowledge of the native cure used in the St. Lawrence region had apparently been lost. Of the 79 men who overwintered, 35 died. Indians brought some relief with fresh moose meat in March, but about twenty more men were close to death when an anxiously awaited supply ship arrived from France in mid-June. Among the dead were the constantly sparring Catholic and Protestant clerics. One story relates that the survivors purposely, and no doubt with some humour, buried them in the same grave in the hope that, in death, they might share a closeness they had not enjoyed in life.

After five weeks exploring the coastline to the south as far as Cape Cod in the hope of finding a better location for settlement, Champlain and de Monts returned, dissatisfied, to St. Croix in early August. With time running out before winter, they decided to take another look at Port Royal, almost directly across the bay. Champlain and Pont Grave re-explored the shoreline of this wide basin and determined a site for settlement, one that offered good prospects for development and was defensible. Equally important was the fact that it was a south-facing location, well-sheltered from the bitter north-west winds of winter by a small mountain. It was opposite an island, now known as Goat Island, past which a large, well-stocked river, named by them L'Equille, flowed from the heart of an inviting valley. The soil was quite fertile, there was an ample supply of fresh water close by, the surrounding forests afforded a plentiful supply of wood and were populated with various species of wildlife, including large moose and deer. Their chances of survival appeared far better here than they had been at St. Croix.

Men were put to work clearing the area of trees while others set to dismantling buildings on the island across the bay. It took several trips to complete the move. When the building work at the Port Royal Habitation, adapted from the design of a fortified French manor house, was nearing completion, de Monts set sail for France to personally report to the King on developments, while Pont Grave agreed to stay at Port Royal to oversee the activities of the remaining 45 Frenchmen. Champlain also remained behind, determined to carry out further exploration along the coast.

When finished, the Habitation contained a trading store, forge, bakery, and a chapel, in addition to living quarters. Although it was late in the season, several gardens plots were dug and planted with a variety of vegetables, an activity in which Champlain energetically participated. To everyone's delight and pleasure, the soil produced quickly and abundantly.

In spite of the heavy workload, many of the men took the opportunity to share and learn about each other's tasks, to freely garden and fish, and to generally enjoy a liberality among themselves that would have been improbable back in Europe. With the new land came a new mindset, and it showed itself in small ways early on at Port Royal.

The extensive activities of the Frenchmen at Port Royal quickly brought them in direct contact with the native population, whom they called Souriquois, but who later became known as Mi'kmaq. Almost totally unfamiliar with the geography of the area beyond the Habitation's fortified wooden walls, the Frenchmen were very much aware that they were strangers in another's territory, and that danger existed for them daily, not just from the elements and wildlife, but possibly also from a native population that had, in other places, violently opposed European settlement. At Port Royal, such fears turned out to be groundless. The Mi'kmaq who fished and hunted in Acadie had already benefited from trade with the white man and they tolerated the oddly dressed strangers who had come across the great sea in wind-blown ships into their river valley. From a distance, they watched them as they built their impressive encampment, worked with metal tools, and hunted with powerful weapons.

Meanwhile, back in France, de Monts, in the face of the previous year's poor financial returns and continuous opposition to his charter, was struggling to raise additional investment to sustain the settlement for at least another year. De Monts' charter was opposed by many French merchants fearful of losing their cut of the lucrative fishery and fur trade. King Henri's decree of religious tolerance, noble and necessary as it was, did not by any means end the animosity between Catholic and Protestant, and the Huguenot de Monts' appointment was resented in certain quarters. Although he had been granted a ten-year monopoly of trade, he had no way of enforcing it against the scores of sailors who annually traded with native tribes. To these seafaring entrepenuers, de Monts' charter was an infringement on their independence and a threat to their hard-won livelihood. He decided to remain in France for the time being, as much for political as for commercial reasons.

It was early spring of 1606 before a vessel could be fitted out, new settlers found, and supplies purchased. Poutrincourt, who had expressed his admiration for Port Royal on first seeing it, willingly took over as Governor at de Monts' request, and was finally able to sail in mid-May. On board the 150-ton *Jonas* with him were his son Biencourt and Marc Lescarbot, a literary lawyer who was more than pleased with the opportunity to escape from what he felt was the superficial life of Paris. The voyage, however, almost ended in failure. The late arrival of the *Jonas* at Port Royal at the end of July after a slow crossing came just in time to prevent the Habitation from being abandoned. By mid-June, neither de Monts nor Poutrincourt had returned from France, and with supplies running dangerously low, the anxious Pont Grave had two small vessels built to transfer the members of the party back to Canseau or Gaspé, where they likely would be able to find passage home on a French fishing boat. When no relief vessel had arrived by July 16, 1606, all but two of the remaining members of France's first settlement in continental North America left Port Royal. The pair who stayed behind to guard the Habitation, its contents, and the remaining stores were promised 50 crowns each and the assured protection of Memberto, the Mi'kmaq chief. Pont Grave and his departing party were fortuitously intercepted as they sailed along the south shore of Nova Scotia and gladly returned to join their compatriots at Port Royal. Lescarbot immediately became enchanted by the air, the idyllic environment, and the natural abundance. His overflowing appreciation of what Acadie had to offer was expressed in poetry, song, and drama, which he shared with others back in France in his *Historie de la Nouvelle France*, published in 1609.

Poutrincourt was determined to make the settlement, to which he was heavily committed philosophically and financially and where he intended to relocate his entire family, as active and productive as possible. Although fur trading and mining were still the intended sources of financial return, Poutrincourt's more personal plans included developing Port Royal into a self-sufficient agrarian community, to which other war-weary Frenchmen and their families might be attracted. The fertile soil of the area was impressive, as the late-sown produce of the previous year had shown. Ground was now prepared for the first planting of European grains in Canada and, within weeks of sowing, the soil began to produce wheat and rye, as Lescarbot noted with amazement in his journal.

It was now obvious that a productive agricultural community could be developed on the shores of this basin and farther upriver. With this in mind, Poutrincourt had additional buildings constructed the following spring, in anticipation of the arrival of new settlers. Because the grinding by hand of the settlement's wheat had been so laborious during the winter months, Poutrincourt ordered construction of a water mill. After scouting a smaller, winding river that flowed into the L'Equille, a suitable location was found about three kilometres inland and an impressive mill quickly built. It was the first such structure in Canada and, with its large water-driven wheel moving the heavy grinding stones, it aroused great curiosity among the Mi'kmaq, who were already impressed by the strong metallic tools and weapons of the French. Water power and the beginning of the mechanical age had arrived on the North American continent.

During the spring of 1607, Poutrincourt, Champlain, and a few others sailed south again to explore the Maine coastline, and the almost six-week absence of several of the leading members of the settlement fostered some anxiety and unrest among some of the remaining men. Lescarbot noted that there was a strong possibility some might mutiny and take over the fledgling colony by force or abandon it altogether. In anticipation of his colleagues' safe return and to calm fears and relieve tensions, Lescarbot penned and prepared a stylized poetic pageant entitled *Theâtre de Neptune*. This play, the first such production in Canada, was presented in front of the Habitation to his enthusiastic fellow countrymen and to what must have been the amused bewilderment of the native Mi'kmaq.

Of course, living conditions had improved from year to year, and now social life was boosted by the creation of *L'Ordre de Bon Temps* (The Order of Good Cheer) in which these Gallic epicureans created Canada's first gourmet feast. Its fourteen members took turns acting as chief steward and hosting the others. Natural rivalry and camaraderie ensured that the members of the Order, at times including Memberto and other neighbouring chiefs, enjoyed sumptuous meals, ceremoniously served, throughout the dreary months of winter. Lescarbot, in reply to later criticism in France about the diet at the

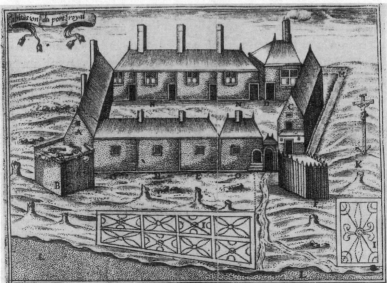

Samuel de Champlain's "picture plan" of the Habitation at Port Royal

Habitation, replied that they enjoyed as good a table as could be served in the best Paris restaurants, and at a fraction of the cost.

Poutrincourt's was at pains to keep the fledgling settlement free of religious conflict, and no clerics were brought from France the second year. Missionary sentiments notwithstanding, no serious measures were taken to convert the native population to Christianity, at least for the time being. In the absence of a church representative, the learned and adaptable Lescarbot undertook responsibility for lay religious services at the Habitation.

Just as the settlement's leading figures were beginning to think they had succeeded in establishing a permanent place for themselves and other Frenchmen in Acadie, they received disastrous news. On May 24, 1607 a small French ship arrived in the harbour, its young captain carrying with him a letter of instruction from de Monts to Poutrincourt. The ten-year charter issued by the King only two years earlier had been suddenly revoked. No further finances could be raised to support the settlement, and Port Royal was to be abandoned. They were to leave Acadie and return to France as soon as possible.

On July 30th, after a large stock of furs and skins had been acquired in trade with area Indians, Lescarbot left Port Royal in two small vessels, along with the artisans, tradesmen, and other labourers. Poutrincourt stayed behind for a few weeks, waiting for the crops to ripen so he could bring samples of the soil's productivity back to France. Leaving no stone unturned in his effort to win a reprieve for Port Royal, he made one last attempt to find mines in what has come to be known as Minas Basin. He and a few others, including Champlain, scoured the coastline in search of further evidence of valuable ores, and many rock samples were collected. Finally, on August 11, 1607 the French presence in Acadia came to a temporary end after three years of tragedy and triumph. Leaving the Habitation and its gardens to the care of the local Mi'kmaq chief Memberto, Poutrincourt and Champlain sailed out of the beautiful basin.

When he got back to Paris, Poutrincourt was faced with accusations that too much time and money had been spent on the Habitation and insufficient effort made to establish profitable trade with the Indians. He was also reminded that there had not been any serious attempt to convert them to Christianity. Nonetheless, he petitioned the King for an extension of the grant originally given to de Monts. In spite of the risk of alienating both powerful merchants and the Catholic church, the King agreed to Poutrincourt's request and extended de Monts' charter for one more year, on condition that he establish a permanent trading post in New France.

De Monts lost little time in winning over the support of various merchants in such ports as Rouen, St. Malo, and La Rochelle, and he soon had enough money to procure and equip three ships. He decided to send Champlain and Pont Grave in two ships to the St. Lawrence region and leave the third ship for Poutrincourt to take back to Port Royal.

This one-year extension brought Champlain unexpectedly back to Québec in June of 1608, where he survived yet another terrible winter during which almost half of his 28 companions died. It also allowed Champlain to pursue his three-fold mission of winning the goodwill of the Indian population of the region, expanding the French fur trade, and exploring the unknown interior of the continent. Henri's extension led directly to the development of a permanent French presence in the country.

Detained in France by legal and financial matters, Poutrincourt was not able to sail for Port Royal until February of 1610. He had agreed to the King's request to have the native population instructed in Christian teachings, but he did not want to involve the Jesuits, of whom he was deeply suspicious. He corresponded with the Pope, who arranged for a secular priest, a Fr. Flesche, to travel with him to Acadie.

After a trip filled with many delays, Poutrincourt arrived at Port Royal in late April. On board once again was his son, Biencourt, his merchant and cousin, Claude de La Tour and his son Charles, apothycarist Louis Hebert, Fr. Flesche, and a small group of artisans and farm labourers. They immediately began repairing and cleaning up the neglected Habitation and planted the nearby gardens and fields with a variety of vegetables and grains.

Poutrincourt's son, Biencourt, returned to France in July, intending to bring out additional winter supplies for the two dozen men at Port Royal. Arriving back in France in August, he was horrified to learn that Henri IV had been assassinated on May 14th, 1610 by a religious fanatic. France was once again in a state of religious and political turmoil.

The new King, Louis XIII, was still a boy of eight and matters of state were being handled by his mother, Marie de Medici, who, to the disgust of France's Huguenot population, favoured her Italian relatives and the Jesuits. On the prompting of one of her ladies-in-waiting, the attractive and financially secure widow Madame de Guercheville, who was a devout Catholic, the Queen Mother decreed that two Jesuits should accompany the young Biencourt back to Acadie to take charge of the mission work among the native population. Sharing his father's view of the Jesuits, he tried to leave without his two unwanted passengers, but the Queen Mother intervened, and the Jesuits, Fr. Baird and Fr. Masse, embarked with him in late January, 1611 on a long, cold, and stormy voyage that brought them to Port Royal in May.

Greatly disturbed by the Jesuits' presence and the influence they would exert on the future of the settlement, Poutrincourt hastened back to France to try to maintain his control over Port Royal, where about twenty men were still actively working. His persistent objections at court to the Jesuits, combined with the hostility that had grown between Biencourt and the pair at Port Royal, finally resulted in Madame de Guercheville supporting the Jesuits' decision to establish another settlement elsewhere. She succeeded in purchasing from the cash-strapped de Monts, who was preoccupied with Champlain's settlement in Québec, all of the Acadian lands covered by his charter, with the sole exception of Port Royal. With Poutrincourt now languishing in debtors' prison, she used her extensive wealth to provision another ship with fresh supplies and more Catholic settlers. Leaving the port of Honfleur in March 1613, it reached Port Royal in May, picked up the two Jesuits, then sailed on to the coast of present-day Maine, where the new settlement of Ste. Sauveur was begun on Mount Desert Island.

A few weeks later the people of the new settlement were surprised to see an English ship approaching. It was the *Treasurer*, commanded by privateer Captain Samuel Argall, who had been sent north by the Governor of the English colony at Jamestown with 60 soldiers to remove any French from what the British had long considered their territory. The landings of John Cabot were the basis of the English claim to the continent and, in their minds, the French had no right to be where they were. After brave resistance that resulted in two deaths and several woundings, the Ste. Sauveur settlers were captured and taken back to Virginia.

In October, Argall came north again, having learned about Port Royal, and Biencourt, from his captives. It is said that Fr. Baird personally guided the ship to the location of his sworn enemy. When Argall sailed into the basin on November 1, 1613 with orders to destroy the settlement and dispatch the French, he found the Habitation almost deserted, the men busy hunting or working in the fields upriver. Hoping to retain the dwellings, and possibly aiming to get his hands on Fr. Baird, Biencourt hastily began negotiations, but Argall refused to compromise, and the buildings that had been built in 1605 were stripped and destroyed. After a final warning to the French that they were occupying English territory, Argall returned to Virginia.

Poutrincourt, who had somehow managed to raise fresh funds in France and free himself from jail, had set sail for Port Royal in late December of 1613 with a shipload of supplies. Arriving at Port Royal in late March, he found his dream in ruins and the remaining French struggling to survive among the Mi'kmaq. After deciding it was impossible to remain, he regretfully returned to France, only to die while fighting for the King in December, 1615. His son Biencourt, along with the La Tours and a few other men, decided to stay in Acadie, living much like the Mi'kmaq, by fishing, hunting, and trading furs with visiting French ships. In later years, the enterprising Biencourt established trading posts at Port Royal, at the mouth of the Saint John River, and near Cape Sable Island, but by the time of his death in 1623 there was no longer any official French presence in Acadie. The French Crown seemed to have simply lost interest in it.

Through a strange twist of historical fate, Claude de La Tour, who gained a thorough knowledge of the Acadian coast, would play

Monument to Sieur de Monts overlooking the Annapolis Basin

an important part in guiding the Alexander settlers to the basin at Port Royal. His son Charles, having been bequeathed territory by Biencourt in Acadie, left his own mark on its history.

Although the buildings were gone, the gardens overgrown, and the project abandoned, something of the faith of the founders of Port Royal, of their vision of its future and of the determination with which they tried to realize their dreams remained behind, reflected in words carved on the broken, wooden plaque that once adorned the arched entrance to the Habitation. Below the decorative emblem of France were the family mottoes of both de Monts and Poutrincourt: "To these toils too God will give an end" and "To valour no path is pathless."

These noble sentiments equally applied to the dreams and endeavours of the members of the Charlesfort expedition who were to sail into the deserted basin a few years later.

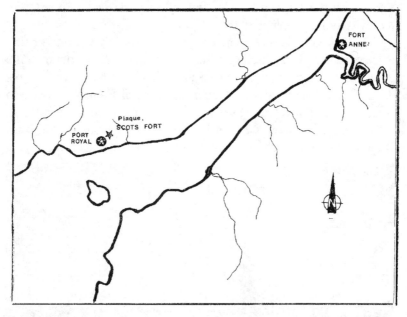

Map by Birgitta Wallace Ferguson, showing the location of the plaque commemorating the "Scots fort" and Fort Anne, the site of the present-day Charlesfort excavation.

10

A New Scotland

Having being born and raised in Scotland, a country almost totally surrounded by the sea and with a history filled with exciting tales of seafaring explorers, William Alexander probably grew up with some awareness of the heroic trans-Atlantic voyages of the past. Tales of the maritime adventures of medieval monks, the stories of Viking adventures, fishermen's talk of western lands, and the exploits of other pre-Columbian mariners all had a place in popular lore, and Alexander may have imbibed of some of them. Whatever historical or legendary material Alexander may have been exposed to in Scotland, on reaching London he must have learned of the adventurous exploits of Elizabethan explorers such as Martin Frobisher, Sir Humphrey Gilbert, John Davys, and Sir Walter Raleigh. The daring accomplishments of Hawkins, Drake, and Cavendish were the talk of the streets. He may have picked up an early copy of Richard Hakluyt's *The Principal Navigations, Voyages and Discoveries of the English Nation*, which contained numerous stories of seamen who had made it across the Atlantic. He would certainly have known of the successful developments of the Virginia Company and the North Virginia Company, formed just prior to his arrival at the English court and which had been granted charters by King James I. These companies involved notable members of the aristocracy, such as the literary-minded Earl of Southampton, believed to have been one of Shakespeare's early patrons, and others with whom Alexander must have had more than a passing acquaintance.

Following Samuel Argall's ousting of the French from the northeastern coast of North America, (a few hardy Frenchmen such as Biencourt and La Tour remained quietly and independently active in Acadie) Englishmen began to ponder settlements of their own there.

With the Jamestown colony securely on its way, the enterprising and intrepid John Smith continued to serve the cause of English colonization. Sailing north, he charted the coastline of Massachusetts and Maine and gave the area the name of New England. Around 1614, Englishmen made an unsuccessful attempt to settle the region. Then, in 1615, the Dutch appeared, started trading with Indians near Albany, and succeeded in making a treaty with the Iroquois. For a few years, it appeared the Dutch would become the fourth European power in North America, but it was not to be. In 1618, an English and Scottish religious sect known as Brownists decided they would be better off on the other side of the Atlantic and applied for permission to establish their own settlement in Virginia. After crossing the Atlantic, their ship the *Mayflower* was blown off course by adverse weather conditions and the group of Puritans landed on the coast of Massachusetts rather than at their intended destination farther south. They made landfall at Provincetown on the tip of Cape Cod and, after crossing the bay, decided they were destined by God to make their stand at a spot they called Plymouth. So began the influx into that region of determined, hard-working, no-nonsense settlers whose faith and sense of community, although not appealing to everyone, would help them survive the many trials and hardships to come.

John Mason had run successful fishing operations out of Newfoundland, and on returning to England in 1620, he published *A Brief Discourse on Newfoundland*. It appears that Mason had had earlier dealings with Sir William, and his book may have sparked Alexander into new-world plans of his own.

Already drawn into Newfoundland adventures was the mystical Welsh poet Sir William Vaughan, a contemporary of Alexander's. This well-educated, idealistic man of letters conceived the idea of contributing to the solution of pressing Welsh economic problems by establishing a settlement, which he called Colchos, at Renews on the Avalon Peninsula. In a publication to which he unabashedly gave the symbolic title *The Golden Fleece*, Vaughan called on others to do their part to help mitigate England's social ills, but few took him seriously and not more than two or three other aristocratic intellectuals joined him in his patriotic enterprise. Unfortunately for Vaughan, most of his settlers declined to indulge in the demanding work expected of them. Alexander would later commiserate with him on the ignoble failure of his well-intentioned experiment.

One of those who responded to Vaughan's call to use colonization to solve British domestic problems was Sir Richard Whitbourne, who, having been with Gilbert when he took possession of St. John's Harbour for England in 1583, was a seasoned man of the sea. He was also an incurable romantic who once claimed he had been approached by a mermaid in St. John's Harbour. Others who acquired land from Vaughan for the purpose of setting up their own colonies were Lord Falkland, who had been involved with the Virginia Company, and the future Lord Baltimore, Sir George Calvert. Both men had already distinguished themselves in government service, and Baltimore now showed his commitment to the colonial cause by moving with his wife and family to Newfoundland. An educated man of vision, he named his holding Avalon, after the royal site made famous in Arthurian legend. A converted Catholic, he later petitioned the King for a separate colony for others of his faith and was given territory north of Virginia. He named it Maryland, after the Catholic queen of the same name.

By the time of Mason's 1620 return from Newfoundland to England, Alexander had completed most of his major literary works. With the Jamestown colony expanding and trade with the new world developing, a tangible atmosphere of unlimited potential surrounded the whole business of trans-Atlantic adventuring. All London was talking about England's growing power overseas. It was perhaps inevitable that the exciting talk at court, the traffic in exotic goods, and the numerous publications about the still mostly unexplored continent would fascinate Alexander's keen mind and stir his active imagination. Many of his powerful court colleagues were directly involved in England's overseas enterprises and, as a close confidant of the King, Alexander was as well placed as anyone to avail himself of the opportunity to get involved.

After reading Mason's work about the attractions of Newfoundland, Alexander invited him to a meeting at his Covent Garden residence in London. The meeting, which had historic repercussions for Nova Scotia, was later described by Sir Ferdinando Gorges, another aristocratic trans-Atlantic adventurer:

"Captain John Mason was himself a man of action and had been sometime Governor of a plantation in the NewFoundLand. His time being expired there he returned to England where he met with Sir William Alexander who was Master of Requests to His Majesty for the realm of Scotland but since Earl of Stirling. Hearing of Captain Mason's late coming out of NewFoundLand was desirous to be acquainted with him. To that end he invited him to his house, and after he had thoroughly informed himself of the estate of that country, he declared his affection to Plantation and wished the Captain to be the means to procure him a grant of the Planters thereof for a portion of the land with them, who effected what he desired."

In consequence of this meeting, land west of Placentia Bay was given to Alexander so he might establish a settlement of his own, to which he gave the name Alexandria. But the matter did not end there, as Gorges relates:

"The Captain understanding how far forth I had proceeded in the business of New England advised him to deal with me for a part of what we might conveniently spare, without our prejudice within the bounds of our grant. Sir William Alexander, intending to make himself sure of his purpose, procured his Majesty to send to me to assign him a part of our territories."

On November 3, 1620 the North Virginia Company was reorganized and given a new patent by King James I as "the Council established at Plymouth in the County of Devon for the planting, ruling, ordering and governing of New England in America." Its extended charter now included lands stretching as far north as Cape Breton and those occupied by the French in the lower St. Lawrence.

Gorges and other advocates of British colonization were more than favourable to the idea of having a new settlement of loyal Protestant subjects, be they Scottish or English, located somewhere between New England and the Catholic colonists in New France. Alexander, seeing an opportunity to advance his own and his native country's interests, seized the moment. In what seems to have been his first conception of a New Scotland in North America he wrote:

"Being much encouraged hereunto by Sir Ferdinando Gorges and some others of the undertakers for New England, I shew them that my countriemen would never adventure in such an Enterprise unless it were, as there was a New France, a New Spain and a New England, that they might likewise have a New Scotland... which they might hold of their owne Crowne, and where they might be governed by their owne Lawes."

Although there obviously were personal motives involved, Alexander also had his nation's and his fellow countrymen's interests at heart in his proposal for a New Scotland. He understood the Scots' need to feel themselves a nation apart from England and also knew the conditions under which many of his fellow countrymen were struggling. There had recently been a serious famine in parts of Scotland that accentuated other social ills. As well, the French were hinting at reclaiming Acadie. Sir William approached his friend the King on the subject, and James I, struggling to come to terms with the unpredictable and tempestuous French on one hand and the impoverished and undisciplined Scots on the other, reacted enthusiastically to the idea of a New Scotland. That he admired and respected Alexander for his artistic and administrative abilities there can be little doubt: that their common interest in literature, Masonic matters, and the possibility of rich returns had a bearing on the wholehearted support Alexander received at court, cannot be discounted. Described by Scottish historian Charles Rogers as "fertile in device and expert in execution and of an unswerving tenacity of purpose," Alexander obviously made good use of the many threads that linked him providentially and favourably to the King. James quickly instructed those in charge of the New England colony to relinquish a large part of their holdings to his Master of Requests for Scotland. Gorges succinctly recorded the proceedings:

> "His majesties gracious message was to me as a command agreeing with his pleasure to have it so. Whereupon an instrument was presently drawn for the bounding thereof, which was to be called New Scotland, which afterward was granted him by the King under the Seal of Scotland. Thus much I thought fit to insert by the way, that posterity might know the ground from whence business of that nature had their original."

The territory of this New Scotland embraced not only present-day Nova Scotia but also New Brunswick, Prince Edward Island, and part of both Québec and Maine. The grant was a proprietary one, giving Alexander sole responsibility for the settlement and development of the territory, which he could do in any number of ways. The new domain was to be administered by Alexander himself on behalf of James as King of Scotland, and all settlers were to have the full rights of citizens of the Crown. As with the previous settlements in

Virginia and Newfoundland, this one had to be privately funded, but unlike them, Alexander's was financed solely from his own coffers. No company of merchant-adventurers was formed to carry the considerable cost of the venture.

James, who seems to have genuinely believed in the future benefits of a New Scotland, both to the impoverished people in the northern part of his domain and to himself, lost little time in instructing his Scottish Privy Council in the following letter dated August 5, 1621:

"Right trusty and well beloved cousins and counsellors and right trusty and well beloved counsellors, Wee greete you well. Having ever beene ready to embrace anie good occasion whereby the honour or proffete of that our Kingdome might be advanced, and considering that no kynd of conquest can be more easie and innocent than that which doth proceede from Plantationes, specially in a country commodious for men to live inà considering how populous that our Kingdome is at this present, and what necessity there is of some good meanes wherby ydle people might be employed preventing worse courses, Wee think there are manie that might be spared who may be fitt for such a forreaine Plantatione, being of mynds as resolute and of bodyes as able to overcome the difficulties that such adventurers must at first encounterà it doth crave the transportation of nothing from thence, but only men, women, cattle and victualls, and not of money, and maie give a good returne of other commodityes, affording the means of a new trade at this tyme when traffic is so much decayed. For the causes above specifeit, Wee have the more willingly harkened to a motion made unto us by our trusty and well beloved Counsellor, Sir William Alexander, Knight, who hath a purpose to procure a forraine Plantation, haveing made choice of landes lying betweene our Colonies of New England and Newfoundland, both the Governors whereof have encouraged him thereuntoà Our pleasure is, that after due consideratione, if you find this course, as Wee have conceaved it to be, for the good of that our Kingdome, that yow grant unto the sayd Sir William, his heires and assignes, or to anie other that will joyne with him in the whole, or in any part thereof, a signatour under our Great Seale of the said lands lying betweene New England and Newfoundland, as we shall designe them particularly unto yow, to be holden for us from our Kingdom of Scotland as a part thereofà And likewise Our pleasure is that you give all the lawful ayde that can be afforded for the furthering of this enterprysee, which Wee will esteeme of good service done to us."

A warrant for Alexander's charter was issued at Windsor Castle on September 10, 1621, and on September 29th the charter itself passed under the Great Seal, appointing Sir William Alexander as the King's hereditary Lieutenant-General of all lands and seas lying roughly between latitudes 43° and 47°N. It was bound by an imaginary border running west from Cape Sable to the mouth of the St. Croix River, north to the St. Lawrence, then east to the Gaspé, out to the tip of Cape Breton, and southwest back to Cape Sable. Embracing numerous coastal islands along the way, it covered some 150,000 square kilometres.

His unique charter gave the 54-year-old poet, playwright, and courtier powers unequalled by any other colonizer in Europe or the new world at the time. James had been generous to his Master of Requests for Scotland, making him virtual king of a vast new domain. Alexander was given authority to exercise full powers in everything ranging from the drawing up of a constitution and laws necessary for the good government of the territory to the development of its natural resources. Alexander was his own Lord of the Admiralty, Chief Justice, Minister of Trade, and Chief of the Exchequer. He could divide and dispose of any part of his grant in any way he wished, negotiate peace or declare war whenever he thought necessary, and declare martial law in case of revolt or rebellion. He was empowered to appoint his own administrators and officers of state and to establish provinces, baronies, towns, villages, and ports. At the same time, all loyal settlers were guaranteed the full privileges of citizens of the Crown and the protection of the laws of Scotland.

To help New Scotland in its commercial growth, it was exempted from import and export duties on all goods for seven years. Alexander held rights to all the fisheries, and could levy taxes and custom duties and prosecute interlopers as he deemed appropriate. To the private fishing interests of the west coast of England and elsewhere, this spelled trouble, and they were prepared to do everything necessary to circumvent or even sabotage Alexander's newly acquired authority over such a lucrative resource. In danger of incurring royal wrath if accused of subverting the authority and wishes of the King by openly opposing Alexander's charter, they may have resorted to more subtle tactics.

Top on the list of the mineral resources both he and the King hoped would be found in New Scotland were gold and silver. James, who was to receive a royalty of ten percent of all wealth uncovered, could be confident that Alexander's previous involvement in mining and refining operations in Scotland would be put to good use in New Scotland. Alexander was authorized to mint coins and regulate the money supply of the new colony, indicating that there was a distinct possibility that gold or silver might be found there. Alexander, who would have known through the court spy network about the earlier efforts of the Frenchmen de Monts and Poutrincourt, certainly hoped mineral wealth would be found, and he and James may even have been privy to private information about such a possibility. It cannot be ruled out that, with James desperately in need of money and with many in Parliament rising in opposition to him, Alexander may have intentionally gone it alone in the hope of directly helping his King should gold be discovered in Nova Scotia. The lengths to which James, and later Charles I, went to support Alexander in his enterprise were extraordinary, and could indicate that there was some quiet arrangement at work whereby any valuable ore found would go to support the beleaguered monarchy, of which Alexander was a most dedicated supporter. Pirates and privateers had used Nova Scotian waters for over 100 years, when men like Hawkins, Drake, and the Dutchman Piet Heyn captured fortunes in gold and silver from Spanish ships leaving Central America. It has never all been accounted for, so it is not unlikely that Alexander had silent partners — if not from the beginning, then later on — with whom he planned to retrieve a treasure. As discussed in my book *Oak Island Secrets*, Alexander may have been involved with a Masonic circle of literary and court associates with whom he engaged in the secret business of concealing a treasure of some kind on Oak Island. He certainly had the opportunity, the experience, and the expertise to initiate and carry out such a plan. Some new evidence may soon be discovered that will shed new light on, and finally solve, this mystery.

Alexander, with the stroke of the royal pen and for the symbolic payment of one Scottish penny every Christmas Day, had become the supreme ruler of a vast new domain. His charter, written in Latin,

Plaque commemorating the 300th anniversary of the issuance of the Charter for Nova Scotia

as was normal for the time, had a decorative cover with an illustration of King James seated on his throne in the act of handing the charter for "Provincae Novae Scotiae" over to Sir William.

Little did Alexander or James know at the time of the long struggle that would be involved in trying to bring the promise of this historic document to life. And little do we yet know of the attempts made to send settlers to Nova Scotia during the first years after the issue of the charter. The facts known today remain few and far between.

Competent and effective as Alexander was as an administrator and statesman, the prospect of single-handedly taking charge of the settling of such a vast territory must have seemed daunting. Nonetheless, this novice but determined colonizer, unaided by others, lacking in both practical knowledge and first-hand experience of the terrain and the challenges it presented, and supporting the venture from his own purse, focussed his considerable faculties on the task at hand. More used to composing a poem and round-table diplomacy, Alexander now launched out on a whole new phase of his life.

Having obtained his charter, the enthusiastic Alexander quickly arranged with his friend, Sir Robert Gordon of Lochinvar, owner of lands adjacent to Solway Firth on Scotland's southwest coast, to take over the whole of Cape Breton as a barony to be called New Galloway. But that was as far as Alexander's redistribution of his lands went, at least for the time being.

Within six months of receiving his charter, Sir William procured a ship in the port of London. It left the capital in March of 1622 to sail to Kirkcudbright on the southwest coast of Scotland. Alexander had chosen that port partly because it was controlled by Sir Robert Gordon, and so he might the sooner get the settlers he needed, but also, according to his own words, "that the business might beginne from the Kingdome, which it doth concerne." The ship didn't reach the small Scottish port until early May, perhaps because of bad weather.

Although the charter made it clear that all those emigrating to New Scotland were entitled to all the liberties and privileges of free and native subjects of the Crown, the inducements of land were not very encouraging. Here, the lack of considerable financial backing had its first negative effect. Land could only be held by those who could afford to purchase it — with the exception of artisans, who were to receive free holdings but could not hand them on to family members after death. Poor farmers wanting to try their luck on virgin trans-Atlantic soil could obtain only leases. These conditions did not offer enough incentive to persuade Scots to leave hearth and home, no matter how humble they were, for an uncertain and insecure future in New Scotland. Not surprisingly, would-be settlers did not flock to the Kirkcudbright dockside. Only one artisan, a blacksmith, and one educated person, a Presbyterian minister, consented to join the handful of agricultural labourers on the first expedition. This lack of enthusiasm for the project may also have been the result of a recent plague. To compound Alexander's problems, provisions were in short supply and those that were available had risen considerably in price.

In spite of this initial shortfall in willing emigrants and the problems with supplies, the first settlers courageously set sail for New Scotland in June, 1622. With a mixture of heavy hearts and high hopes, they watched the familiar green hills of Galloway fade behind them as the small wooden vessel manoeuvred its way into open waters. However, for some unknown reason, presumably either adverse weather, problems with the ship itself, or with some of the crew or passengers, the ship put in at the Isle of Man, where it remained until sometime in early August. Only then did it proceed on its way into the unpredictable waters of the Atlantic. This fragile craft, the name of which remains a mystery to this day and whose captain is also unknown to us, managed to make it across the vast stretch of ocean. After what must have been a nerve-wracking and very uncomfortable experience for the people on board, most of whom had never been to sea before and were inadequately dressed for such a journey, St. Peter's Island off the south coast of Newfoundland was sighted around the middle of September.

Sailing westward, the wave-weary settlers were in sight of the coast of Cape Breton when driven back by a howling southwester. Running for cover, the captain took the vessel and its almost petrified passengers to the shelter of St. John's Harbour in Newfoundland. Exhausted from their harrowing experience and glad of the hospitality of fishing crews, the tired travellers readily disembarked. After connecting with some pioneers in the area (Baltimore and Vaughan had their settlements just down the coast) Alexander's settlers decided to remain in Newfoundland for the winter while the ship made a hasty return to Britain for fresh supplies and to carry news of developments back to Alexander. The first winter in the new world for these would-be Nova Scotians was to be as traumatic as it had been for the first Frenchmen on St. Croix Island eighteen years earlier. One of the coldest winters in years was about to descend on Newfoundland, with tragic consequences for people both innocent of nature's frigid onslaught in this region and hopelessly unprepared for it.

While the settlers were still on their way across the Atlantic, back in London Alexander was about to receive his seal as Chief Justice and Lord of the Admiralty of New Scotland. With an image of the King on both sides, it showed the arms of Scotland and was inscribed appropriately: "for the greater solemnitie in using the said officeis."

Alexander was deeply disappointed to hear that his first expedition, having sighted Nova Scotia, had been unable to get the settlers ashore. Their intended initial destination was probably somewhere along the province's south shore, perhaps in one of the many attractive bays earlier visited by Champlain. Far from being discouraged, Alexander procured, again at his own expense, yet another ship in London, bought fresh supplies, and recruited more colonists. By this time he must have realized that, with his people overwintering in Newfoundland and waiting for more supplies and support, he had no alternative but to follow through.

Alexander, however, found it impossible to respond quickly enough to the urgent needs of those on the other side of the Atlantic. It was late March of 1623 before the *St. Luke* hoisted anchor in the Thames and coasted down into the English Channel. Contrary winds and problems on board, or a combination of the two, kept the vessel in Plymouth Harbour for a whole month. Once again, Alexander experienced the frustration and expense of having his vessel tied up in home waters. It was not until April 28th that the *St. Luke* continued on its voyage, its passengers by now very anxious to be on their way.

It took six weeks to make the crossing, an average time. On June 5th, it arrived in St. John's Harbour in Newfoundland, intending to pick up those who had come out the year before. But eight long months and a fierce winter had passed since the original group of settlers had gone ashore there, and there were terrifying tales told of the hardships endured during the bitter winter months. Lacking proper clothing, living in primitive conditions, and without proper provisions, the settlers had been assaulted by unrelenting winds that carried with them snow and icy rain, the likes of which they had never seen before. For some, the cold was unbearable and they succumbed to a frozen grave. The lack of adequate supplies led to much hunger, severe malnutrition, and the dreaded scurvy. The minister and the blacksmith were among the dead. With the arrival of spring, those who had not dispersed to other Newfoundland settlements had found work in the fishery and the promise of passage home. But the *St. Luke*, with its new faces and fresh supplies, was heartily welcomed and a few of the stop-overs were willing to proceed.

When the *St. Luke* passed Cape Race on June 23rd heading southwest across the Cabot Strait, ten of the original settlers accompanied the new arrivals in the hope of finding a suitable place for settlement somewhere along the Nova Scotia coastline. Given their harrowing winter experience, the prospect of settling in more hospitable terrain to the south must have been irresistible. Fog and contrary winds played havoc with their plans, and it must have seemed to some of them, as they were being blown blindly and fearfully about an unknown sea, that they were being discouraged by providence from ever reaching their goal. After two weeks of helpless wandering through whirling mists, these much-tormented travellers finally sighted Nova Scotia somewhere along the northeast coast of Cape Breton.

Reaching the mainland, the *St. Luke* sailed past Canso and down along the southeast coast of the province. On the lookout for inviting terrain, productive land, and a safe natural harbour, the nervous emigrants by-passed the more rugged eastern shore and the future site of Halifax. Over the next two weeks, they surveyed the south shore and probably explored the wide expanse of Mahone Bay and the opening of Lunenburg Harbour. South of present-day Liverpool, they entered Port Mouton, where de Monts, Champlain, and the French settlers of 1604 had first gone ashore. Finding an inviting natural harbour four leagues farther west, the *St. Luke* dropped anchor and the settlers landed and named the spot St. Luke's Bay. Re-embarking, they sailed farther west to present-day Port Joli, which they noted had a fine harbour and a good river. They then proceeded along the coast as far as Cape Negro near the southern tip of the province before heading back to St. John's. Their coastal reconnaissance had given them a good deal of information about the nature of the landscape and possible settlement sites. It may have been because they were too few in number, or perhaps they had been scared off by the deaths of the previous winter, but they decided to return to England. It is known that at least some of the settlers were strongly opposed to staying and threatened hostilities. After loading up with a cargo of fish to help offset the cost of the voyage, the *St. Luke* returned to London, leaving the reluctant settlers to find passage back across the Atlantic on various fishing vessels.

That the normally even-tempered Alexander was more than a little miffed when he learned what had happened might be putting it mildly. All he had to show for his two years of creative planning and intellectual effort, his investment of time and energy, and his approximately £6,000 bankroll were some comments and maps about parts of the south shore of the province. But at least these comments were encouraging. There were glowing reports from the *St. Luke* about Nova Scotia's coastal landscape. They had looked upon "very delicate meadows with roses white and red" that were capable of growing grains and fruit of every kind. Harbours and rivers were described as teeming with a variety of fish. Nova Scotia was a place where a new life, and a new world, could be started.

To help Alexander with his ever-increasing debt, King James charged the cost of the two failed missions against the royal exchequer, but to Alexander's disappointment, the money was never paid out. Those who controlled England's purse strings were in no mood to hand over a stately sum to a Scottish poet, even if he was a member of the court. Alexander's lack of business savvy, the absence of more practical-minded partners, and his inability to take to sea himself to personally direct and supervise the operation, all put him at a distinct disadvantage. These factors were as much to blame for his financial misfortune, from which he would never recover, as were the adverse weather conditions and other negative factors encountered during the two voyages.

Now in possession of a favourable account of conditions in Nova Scotia, but lacking the financial wherewithal to realize his dream, Alexander, desperate to reverse his misfortune, fell back on the resources he still had. Prompted by earlier similiar publications, and possibly encouraged by his literary friends, he picked up his pen to awaken the spirit of trans-Atlantic adventure and national expansion in the minds and hearts of other Scotsmen. Drawing on his own creative abilities, he wrote a highly interesting document in the history of the settlement of both Nova Scotia and Canada. *An Encouragement to Colonies*, issued in London in 1624, was not only one of the most passionate pieces Alexander ever wrote, it was one of the most poetic and idealistic publications dealing with the settling of North America by Europeans in the early 1600s.

This 47-page rhetorical address to would-be pioneers was no ordinary appeal for the support of his fellow countrymen. Pointing out that, in his opinion, the "discovery" of America was a call to Great Britain by providence, he emphasized that it offered an opportunity to "further the work" of creating an overseas empire. Alexander chronicled in some detail the history of emigration from the days of Abraham, through the cultures of Greece and Rome, to the notable achievements and beneficial consequences of the trans-Atlantic exploits of the Spanish, the French, and, of course, the English. Reiterating the reports he had received about the many attractions Nova Scotia had to offer, he painted a glowing picture of the benefits that awaited courtier and commoner, merchant and missionary alike. With a pointed reference to fellow Scots who had adventured abroad to Russia, Poland, and the Mediterranean to fight in foreign wars and gain themselves a justified reputation for adventure and endurance, he made this patriotic pitch: "When I doe consider with myselfe what things are necessarie for a Plantation, I cannot but be confident that my owne Countreymen are as fit for such a purpose as any men in the world." He listed the advantages and attractions of Nova Scotia as seen by those on the *St. Luke*, including land between two rivers somewhere south of Port Mouton that offered "a very fit place for a plantation, both in regard that it is naturally apt to be fortified, and that all the ground between the two rivers is without wood, and very good fat earth, having several sorts of berries growing thereonà as also some sort of grain as pease. They found likewise in every river abundance of lobster, cockles and other shell fishesà also several sorts of wild fowl." Alexander's meditative outlook is obvious in his suggestion that Nova Scotia could be a wholesome refuge to men and women weary of the hardships, hindrances, and crowded conditions of the world they had known: "Here those that are so disposed, without making a Monastical retreate may injoy the pleasures of Contemplation, being solitary when they will and yet accompanied when they please" and that "they may remember their former dangers and communicate their present joyes."

After bringing to their attention the material and psychological benefits that could be theirs in New Scotland, the profoundly religious Alexander rounded out his appeal with a straightforward reference to the spiritual aspect of the project: "But leaving these worldly respects, the greatest encouragement of all for any true Christian is this, that heere is a very large way of advancing the Gospel of Jesus Christ." He urged his fellow Scots to leave "these dreams of honour and profit, which do intoxicate the brains, and impoison the mind with transitory pleasureà that this might bee our chiefe end, to begin a new life, serving God more sincerely than before, to whom we may draw neere by retyring our selves further from hence."

Although high on poetic eloquence and noble sentiment, *An Encouragement to Colonies* is short on climatic and geographic details and on descriptions of the native population and wildlife. This was as much due to the lack of sufficient contemporary information as it was to any tendency to gloss over anything that might discourage future settlers or be viewed as detrimental to the overall success of the operation. But the work included a historic map, a pertinent visual piece of the promotion package, proudly displaying New Scotland occupying the extensive lands between New England to the south and New France to the north. It was divided into the appropriately named provinces of Alexandria and Caledonia. Alexandria, perhaps named as a projection of his own ambitions and aspirations or to invoke ancient memory, took in all of New Brunswick and parts of Maine and Québec. Caledonia, a name for Scotland, took up present-day Nova Scotia. Identification with the old world was also retained by the renaming of rivers on the map. The St. Croix and the Saint John for instance, were labelled "Tweed" and "Clyde" respectively.

But by his literary accomplishments in the English language, Alexander had unintentionally alienated himself from cultural and political nationalists in Scotland, the very people he now needed to turn his colonization enterprise into a success. And his advancement at the English court as a favourite of King James I didn't add to his popularity at home. He had to contend with jealousies, resentments, and enemies among the existing aristocracy, some of whom considered him little more than an opportunistic upstart. His known support of James' Anglican policies angered well-placed members of the militant Scottish church. Added to this was the fact that his nature was such that he did not mix with the Edinburgh establishment, which more and more viewed him as an intruding lackey of the Londn court. Finally, his all-encompassing Nova Scotia charter was resented by fishing interests on the west coast, so much so that James ordered them not to interfere in what amounted to the King's business.

And so it was not surprising that *An Encouragement to Colonies* drew little response in Scotland. In fact, apart from being praised by some for its fine literary content, it was overwhelmingly ignored. It seemed that the refusal of the exchequer to grant him compensation for losses so far incurred in the venture would be the final nail in Alexander's coffin. However, he was determined and versatile, and he approached the King with yet another plan whereby he hoped some well-intentioned and well-off Scottish nobles might be induced to participate in what he proclaimed to all to be "a momentous historic movement."

11

Nova Scotia Knights

Since ascending to the throne of England in 1603, James I had liberally created knighthoods. In fact, he lost little time in exercising this royal prerogative from the day he received word that England wanted him as King. While travelling in state on his way to London from Edinburgh, his joy and generosity knew no bounds and led to the creation of over 200 instant knights. He was soon to dispense the honour more prudently, as one means among many of replenishing the court's coffers, which he found had been left almost empty by England's long war with Spain. He showered almost compulsory knighthoods on the landed gentry, for a fee, of course. There were also the Golden Knights, an order created to provide revenue, at about £300 a knighthood, to help finance the King's mining operations. More relevant to Alexander's situation was the enormous success of the hereditary order of knights baronets James created in order to both effectively sow Ulster with loyal British settlers and to add to his revenues. Between 1611 and 1622, over 200 Baronets of Ulster were enrolled, at approximately £1,000 each, in return for land grants in the cleared Irish countryside. Such a process of raising revenue was considered normal by the customs of the court and the society of the day. Alexander surmised that the same process could provide financial backing, qualified personnel, and suitably prepared settlers for Nova Scotia.

Having maintained sole control over the project and still trying to finance it himself, Alexander now realized that he could not do it alone, as he readily admitted in his petition to the King in the Fall of 1614:

"No man can accomplish such a Worke by his owne private fortunes... I must trust to be supplied by some publike helps, such as hath beene had in other parts... I doubt not but many

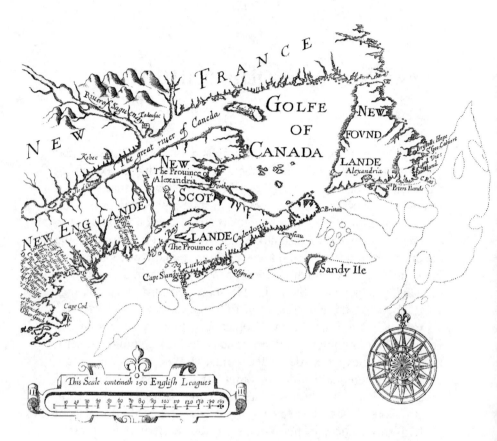

Map drawn by Sir William Alexander for presentation to the Baronets of Nova Scotia in 1624

will be willing out of the noblenesse of their disposition, for the advancing of so worthy a Worke."

He boldly proposed the creation of an order of Baronets of Nova Scotia whereby his colonization project could rapidly and successfully proceed. James, for several reasons, was all ears.

New Scotland, which was already divided into provinces, would be further divided into several dioceses, each diocese into three counties, each county into ten baronies, and each barony into six parishes. Each barony would run sixteen kilometres inland and provide its recipient with at least 16,000 acres. Each would front the sea or a navigable river. The Baronets of Nova Scotia, though not required to reside in their new holdings, would have to "set forth six sufficient men, artificers or labourers, sufficienlie armeit, apparelit and victuallit for two years."

All this seemed so logical, laudable, and perfectly possible that James quickly gave the plan the royal nod. On October 18, 1624 a royal letter was issued from the court to the Scottish Privy Council to the effect that the King had decided to involve himself directly in the colonization of New Scotland. It explained that a new Order of Knighthood, the Baronets of Nova Scotia, was to be created, giving the recipients precedence over all other knights of the realm except those appointed to the honour on the battlefield. The new knights would be addressed as "Sir" on all occasions and the title would be hereditary. James also expressed the view that not only Baronets but the whole Scottish nation would benefit from the settlement of Nova Scotia. The Privy Council was instructed to cooperate by making the King's wishes known to his Scottish subjects. That they did so is obvious from these extracts from their suitably subservient reply of November 23rd:

> "Most Sacred Sovereign, We have considered your Majesty's letter concerning the Baronets and do thereby perceive your Majesty's great affection towards this your ancient kingdom, and your Majesty's most judicious consideration in making choice of so excellent means, both noble and fit, for the good of the same. Wherein seeing your Majesty might have proceeded without our advice and unaquainting us with your Majesty's royal resolution therein, we are so much the more bound to render unto your Majesty our most humble thanks for your

gracious respect unto us... And we humbly wish that this honour of Baronet should be conferred upon none but Knights and
gentlemen of chief respect for their birth place and fortunes,
and we have taken a course by proclamation to make this your
Majesty's gracious intentions to be publicly known that none
hereafter pretending ignorance take occasion inwardly to com-
plain as being neglected... of so fair an opportunity... Therefore our humble desire unto your Majesty is... that the said
number of men be duly transported thither, with all provisions
necessary, and that no Baronet be made but only for that cause,
and by some such one course as only your Majesty shall appoint, and that Articles of Plantation may be set forth for encouraging and inducing anyone who has the ability and
resolution to transport themselves hence for so noble a purpose.... So expecting your Majesty's further direction, and
humbly submitting our opinions to your Majesty's incompara-
ble judgment, we humbly take our leave, praying the Almighty
God to bless your Majesty with a long and happy reign."

A proclamation concerning Nova Scotia was publicly announced at
the Market Cross in Edinburgh on November 30, 1624. Interested
parties, preferably young men of gentle birth and good reputation
and with an income of not less than £900 per year, would have ample
time to weigh their prospects, and then sign up by an intended
deadline of April 1, 1625. Here, any reference to Sir William, the
not-so-popular Master of Requests for Scotland, was noticeably ab-
sent. However, everyone knew who was behind this bid for Baronets,
in spite of the King's active role. Each Baronet, as well as financing
a group of settlers, was also required to pay to Sir William "one
thousand merkis Scottish money towards his past charges and endea-
vouris." (One merk was equal to approximately two-thirds of a
pound.) Although intended as a means of paying down his debt, this
was hardly a tactic that would help him win friends and influence
people, both of which he now desperately needed to do.

Not surprisingly, the appeal drew little immediate response and
by late March of 1625, an anxious Alexander, concerned now about
the very survival of his Nova Scotia project, gained further royal
assent to change some of the conditions of the original proclamation.
The clauses requiring each Baronet to pay Alexander £650 to send
out six men to the colony were dropped. Instead, each Baronet could

cover the cost of settlement by a single payment of 2,000 merks, expenditure of which would be carefully monitored. Alexander no doubt sensed both the frugal nature of his fellow countrymen and their suspicions of him as an agent of the English court. The more favourable conditions were made public on March 23, 1625.

Unfortunately, four days later, before a single knight could be inducted into the order, James I died. On his deathbed, he urged his countrymen to join his illustrious friend Alexander in the creation of a New Scotland, saying that he considered it "a good work, a Royal work and one beneficient to the Kingdome in general."

At this juncture a lesser mortal might have thrown in the towel and walked away from a project that had proven to be not only financially draining and physically exhausting but also the source of much resentment among his fellow countrymen and courtiers. Alexander, however perceived his long-time benefactor's death as an opportunity to revitalize his plans for Nova Scotia through the auspices of the new king, his former pupil, Charles I.

This handsome, bearded, and reserved monarch, suffered as a youth from a physical handicap and a serious speech impediment and so he must have appreciated the considerate ways of his tutor, Alexander. He proved as supportive of the project as his father had been, if not more so. He had, in fact, declared his commitment to Alexander's cause prior to his father's death in a letter to the Scottish Privy

The shields of Nova Scotian Baronets now displayed at Menstrie Castle

Council: "We favour bothe the bussienes and the persone that fol-
loweth it." In spite of his pressing commitments at court and his
almost immediate entanglements with a Parliament highly critical of
royal expenditures and powers, Charles found the time on May 28,
1625 to create the first Nova Scotia knight. The honour was conferred
on Alexander's close friend, Sir Robert Gordon, who would attempt
settlement on Cape Breton. On July 12th, Charles renewed the original Nova Scotia charter to Sir William and also added to the territory
assigned with each knighthood and increased the number of possible
Baronets from 100 to 150.

To encourage more applicants to come forward, they were given
the option of making a single payment to Sir William of 2,000 merks,
with a guarantee that he would apply two-thirds of it to "the setting
forth of a colonie of men furnished with necessarie provision, to be
planted within the said countrie."

The new Baronets were also to be saved the risk and cost involved in a voyage to Nova Scotia to personally take possession of
their new holdings, A ceremony, to be conveniently carried out at
Edinburgh Castle "immediately within the outer gate" on a plot of
ground declared Nova Scotian territory for the purpose, would relieve them of the burden of trans-Atlantic travel. Even the bother of
a trip to court in London could to be avoided, as a special council in
Edinburgh was to be given the authority to dispense the titles. Although these concessions did not result in the hoped-for response, at
least fifteen new knights had joined the ranks by the end of October,
1625. However, this did not raise near enough money to help Alexander deal with his debt, let alone allow him to get another ship
underway.

Pushing the matter further, the King, perhaps at Alexander's
behest, told the Scottish Privy Council in a no-nonsense letter that
they needed to produce more prospective lairds so a shipload of
settlers could sail the following spring for New Scotland. Charles,
not one to mince words or pull punches when it came to a showdown,
emphasized that preference would be given to Nova Scotia knights
in both England and Scotland. In so doing, he salted the sore feelings
and wounded pride of many of the lesser Scottish nobles, who had
little time for Charles' heavy-handed ways in political and religious
matters. They took their anger out on Alexander, who they saw as
the son of a small landowner who had risen too rapidly for his own

good at court, and who stood with the English monarch in everything the Scottish church and political hierarchy opposed.

When the matter of the Nova Scotia charter came before the Scottish Parliament for ratification in November of 1625, a furore erupted that threatened to sink the venture then and there. Members of the old nobility petitioned the Scottish parliamentarians to support an appeal they had made to the King asking him to abandon the charter's preference clause, at least until the settlement had been established as intended. A debate ensued between members of the old nobility and Sir William, with the Scottish lairds objecting to the Nova Scotia Baronets and making the surprise suggestion that they themselves would be willing to undertake the settlement of New Scotland, and at their own expense. The Scottish Parliament, as was to be expected, sided with the lairds, and an appropriately worded petition was duly dispatched to the court in London.

Perhaps sensing early rumblings of the political eruptions in the north that would later topple him from his throne, Charles took his time responding to this dispatch from his disgruntled Scottish subjects. However, in mid-February of 1626, having presumably weighed the pros and cons of the situation, he sent his own missive northward. Carrying the full authority of a king, who like his father before him believed himself to be supreme in the land, it had all the tone and verbiage of a royal rebuke and included a penalty for the perceived leader of those who had so audaciously objected to their monarch's command. The Secretary of State for Scotland, Thomas Hamilton, Earl of Melrose, was summarily removed from office and the position was granted to Sir William. Naturally, such a turn of events did not help endear the already much-resented Alexander to his Scottish colleagues. It also probably added to the difficulties and delays that Alexander was still to experience in getting his New Scotland plans on track again. Before too long, probably at Alexander's request, Hamilton was appeased by being given back part of his lost position and some of its privileges, though the office and title remained Alexander's until his death.

In July of 1626, by which time the uncompromising Charles had dissolved an un-cooperative London Parliament and was trying to raise funds of his own to rule as he thought fit, the King gave further thought to Alexander's colony. He ordered the creation of attractive armorial bearings befitting a country with its own order of knighthood. Set against the backdrop of the Scottish cross of St. Andrew were the ancient arms of the kingdom, on one side of which stood a Mi'kmaq man and on the other a unicorn. Above these an armed hand and a naked one held a laurel branch and a thistle. It was from this historic design that the the present flag and coat of arms of Nova Scotia were later derived.

Preoccupied as he was with matters of state, Alexander maintained his interest in Nova Scotia and, in spite of opposition and financial woes, he remained optimistic he would eventually establish a settlement, as an account of his meeting with Welshman William Vaughan indicates. Just returned from his struggling settlement in the south of Newfoundland, Vaughan was also facing hard times. In Alexander, who invited him to his house, he found a sympathetic and understanding friend. Vaughan later wrote:

> "This learned knight with a joyful countenance and alacrity of mind, taking me by the hand, thus began: I have oftentimes wished to confer with you but until this present I could not find the opportunity. It is necessary, and this necessity jumps from the sympathy of our Constellations, for I think we were both born under the same horoscope, that we advise and devise some Project for the proceedings and successful management of our plantations."

Knowing well of Vaughan's concerns, Alexander summed up their mutual situation:

> "You have spent much and so have I in advancing these hopeful adventures. But as yet neither of us have arrived at the heaven of our expectations... the charge... cannot but grow to an excessive cost. To expect more help than it pleased our most bountifull king already to bestow upon us will bee in vaine, I doubt, considering the scarcity of mony in these dayes."

After commiserating further with Vaughan and referring to the hardships faced and losses incurred by Raleigh and other advocates of colonization, Alexander makes reference to his own failed attempts, his mounting debt, and the hope that the Baronets will be able to come to his rescue, if only partially:

"The like inconveniences I have felt, even in the infancy of my attempt; whether the effects proceeded through the late season of the year, when we sent out the Colony, or by the slowness of our people who, wearied in their passage at sea by reason of contrary winds, rested themselves too long in St. John's Harbour and at my Lord Baltimore's plantation, I knowe not; but sure I am, it cost me and my friends very dear and brought us into much decrements; and has well nigh disheartened my poor Countrymen if, at my humble suit, our most noble and generous King Charles had not, out of his Royal magnificence and respective care to us and our posterities restored and revived our courages by conferring such monies as might arise by the creation of Knights Baronets in Scotland towards the erecting of this new fabrick and heroical action. And yet I fear all this will not suffice and defray the charge."

Undeterred by criticisms and debates, and in spite of insufficient funds, we find Alexander in a letter to the Exchequer of January 17, 1627, referring to the fact that he was then arranging the fitting out of a ship at the port of Dumbarton on the Clyde for yet another attempt to get a Nova Scotia settlement up and running. He assured his inquisitorial financial masters that all money channelled to him was being used for the furtherance of the Nova Scotia colony, and suggested that the ship, its furnishings, and provision be examined to dispel any doubts.

Other factors were also egging him on. The English were more firmly established than ever in North America — in Virginia, New England, and also Bermuda. The Dutch were making inroads of their own in the new world. There were even rumours that France, increasingly under the control of Cardinal Richelieu, who was then commanding the seige of the Protestant port of La Rochelle, had every intention of re-staking its claim to Acadie, now part of the lands covered by the Nova Scotia charter.

But by July of 1627 only about 35 Baronets had been conferred and many of these had not put their money down. There were not enough funds to get ships, settlers, and provisions across the Atlantic. More apprehensive now than ever, Alexander again appealed to Charles. Although immersed in his own financial and political problems, in March of 1628 the King wrote to the Earl Marshal of Scotland exhorting him to expedite payments to Sir William, who in preparing for another expedition to Nova Scotia, "hath been at much more charges than as yet he hath received monies from the knights baronets," and that unless monies owed were forthcoming, Alexander would be "utterly undone in his estate."

France had declared war on England early in 1627 and it was obvious that Alexander could delay no longer. France had become set on overseas expansion, and Cardinal Richelieu, now virtually running France and having enormous wealth at his disposal, had formed the Company of One Hundred Associates for that very purpose. Spies had brought news that an enormous fleet was being prepared to re-assert the French claims in Acadie and in the St. Lawrence region. Alexander had to act now or lose forever the possibility of fulfilling his dream. Several of the Baronets contributed the funds necessary for Alexander to purchase and outfit another vessel to join the one waiting at Dumbarton. By January, 1627 he had obtained two ships to be provisioned in London. However, delays, kept the vessels tied up until early March, and then only one, *The Eagle*, made it norhward. The other was held against a debt of its captain, and it took a royal command to the High Treasurer of England, no doubt at the cash-strapped Alexander's urgent request, to allow it to pass from the Thames free of custom.

Alexander's eldest son, William, had by this time graduated from Glasgow University, been presented at court, and knighted. He was now ready to command the expedition. Several more Baronets came forward, perhaps sensing the urgency of the situation or out of patriotic pride. In the years ahead, their numbers were to swell to over 100. King Charles authorized all members of this new order to wear about their necks a pendant containing the arms of Scotland and the cross of St. Andrew on a silver shield surrounded by the motto *Fax Mentis Honestae Gloria* (Glory is the Torch of a Noble Mind).

By late Spring of 1627, all seemed in place for a final attempt to transport settlers to their new home across the Atlantic, but it was not to be. Hostilities with France and ongoing tensions with Spain made the open seas far too dangerous, and the Atlantic was off-limits to such voyages. All shipping was needed in the war effort, and so once again Alexander's plans for sending settlers to Nova Scotia had to be put on hold.

12

Charlesfort At Last

After France declared war on England in 1627, William Alexander
Jr. was authorized by the King to seize enemy ships. He took the ship
and crew his father had acquired at Dumbarton and struck out on a
privateering voyage. By June, he had returned to Edinburgh, having
gained his sea legs and a prize in the form of the *St. Lawrence* out
of Lubec, which was loaded with salt, a much-needed and remunerative commodity in the fishing trade. All or part of the money raised
from this adventure was intended to go against his father's Nova
Scotia debts. However, penny-pinching members of the Scottish
Treasury, who had recently once again ignored the King's order to
reimburse Alexander for his original expenditures, thought otherwise, and the money ended up in their coffers.

Meanwhile, word had come that Richelieu and his associates
were preparing to send a fleet of ships, a large quantity of armaments
and supplies, and numerous new settlers to Canada in an all-out effort
to establish New France in North America. The senior Alexander and
others feared that this would include the territories granted to him by
James I. The war with France and the news of its renewed interest
in the St. Lawrence region also brought other players onto the field.
A Huguenot merchant, Gervase Kirke, arrived in England from
Dieppe with his sea-going sons and immediately indicated his interest in taking on the French armada, which was sure to offer profitable
spoils, and establishing a settlement somewhere along the St.
Lawrence. Interested in forming a partnership for this purpose, the
Kirkes found the backing they needed among a group of London
traders, and since the Nova Scotia charter included land on the south
shore of the St. Lawrence, they and the Alexanders agreed to band
together in support of each other's interests.

These new arrangements, involving as they did more ships and
manpower, caused additional delay, while eyes and ears searched and
listened anxiously for some indication that the French were them-

selves ready to sail. Delayed at Dumbarton for over six months, some crew members already hired by Alexander grew understandably restless, their drunken antics and insulting behaviour causing annoyance to the good citizens of the town. Alexander himself came in for harsh words because of unpaid wages, and was fortunate not to have to go to the trouble of hiring replacements. Settlers who had agreed to travel got disheartened, returned to their homes, or simply departed.

Then, early in 1628, one of Kirke's sons returned from a reconnaissance mission to the St. Lawrence with the news that the French stronghold of Québec, under the command of the aging Champlain, was poorly manned and could be easily captured. There was no time to lose, and, on March 26, 1628, William Alexander Jr., in command of four vessels, left London for Scotland. On a morning in May, with his mainsail displaying the colourful crest of Nova Scotia, Sir William Jr. (known as Lord William Alexander) and 60 to 70 settlers left Dumbarton to join an unofficial English fleet under command of the Kirkes bound for Canada. By late spring they had safely crossed the Atlantic.

It appears that the settlers were put ashore with supplies and equipment as soon as land was sighted. Exactly where they disembarked is still uncertain, but it was probably at either Tadoussac, which had been easily captured from the French, or on the south shore of Newfoundland, where Alexander still held land and they would be in contact with other British settlers.

After assessing Champlain's situation at Québec, the Kirkes and the young Alexander took on a French naval force sheltering from a storm off the Gaspé Peninsula. Richelieu had spared no expense on this fleet in his determination to establish French supremacy in Canada, but the smaller British ships quickly outmanoeuvred the surprised French vessels. Their commander surrendered, and seventeen ships, complete with their cargoes, crews, and passengers, were captured — a profitable catch and a national triumph for both Alexander and the Kirkes.

The younger Alexander returned with the Kirkes in triumph to England, and his father's happiness at developments was made clear in a letter, dated November 18, 1628, to the Earl of Menteith, President of the Scottish Privy Council: "My son, praised be God, is returned safe, having left a Colony near Canada behind him, and I am dealing for a new setting forth from London."

The success of this voyage made others in England sit up and take notice of the financial benefits to be gained by triumph over the French. In a letter from a William Maxwell of Edinburgh to his cousin Sir John Maxwell, mention was made not only of the settlers left by Alexander, who Maxwell believed were somewhere in Nova Scotia, but also of the mounting pressures at court concerning property jurisdiction and the profit potential of privateering and trade in the St. Lawrence region:

"It is for certain that... William Alexander is come home again from Nova Scotia, and hath left behind him seventy men and two women, with provisions to serve them for the space of one year, being placed in a part of the country which is a natural strength together with some cannon, musket, powder, and bullet, in case of sudden invasion, together with all things necessary for their present use; and is to go hither again in the Spring with a new plantation. But since he came home the English men are requesting his Majesty to plant and possess whatsoever lands thereof which they please, and there to be holden of the Crown of England. What shall be the event I know not."

Lord William spread some of his good fortune around, as is indicated by church records in Stirling. In an entry dated December 25, 1628 it is noted that "Sir William Alexander Jnr., after his return from his sea voyage, gave the poor of Stirling fifty eight pounds."

It was now clear that the St. Lawrence region might yield great riches, and English interests petitioned Charles I to give them sole access to it. But Alexander persuaded the Scottish Privy Council to uphold his claim and it appears that an agreement was reached whereby Alexander not only retained his extensive Nova Scotia holdings but was granted "all the country and coasts within the Gulf of Canada on both sides of the river till they arrive within ten leagues of Tadoussac."

Charles continued to favour his former tutor, now a tried and trusted statesman. In a royal patent dated February 4, 1629, permission was given to all members of an Anglo-Scottish trading alliance headed by Alexander to "make a voyage into the Gulf and River of Canada, and the parts adjacent, for the sole trade of bever wools, beaver skins, furs, hides and skins of wild beasts."

The patent, granted in the name of Lord William Alexander, empowered the alliance to jointly settle plantations "within all parts of [the] gulf and river above those parts which are over against Quebec." The Alexanders were at this point perhaps the most powerful landholders in the whole of North America.

The business of maintaining jurisdiction over his territory, which few had expressed interest in up until then, turned into a wily affair of state now that it was obvious the project could succeed and be extremly lucrative. It required the diligent exercise of all Alexander's diplomatic and political skills to maintain himself at the helm, and there were still the French to contend with. Fortunately for Alexander, the capture of Richelieu's well-financed fleet had almost bankrupted its French backers.

By a remarkable coincidence, among the many French captured by the Kirkes was Claude de La Tour, one of the alumni of the Poutrincourt years at the Port Royal Habitation. Along with his son Charles and a handful of others, he had remained in Acadie after France had abandoned it, living among the Mi'kmaq and trading with French merchant vessels near Cape Sable at the southern tip of Nova Scotia. On hearing of the renewal of French interest in Canada, he and his son made a pitch for official recognition and support in Acadie. He had gone to France to present their case and was returning to Acadie when he was captured. Such were the early fortunes of this war for Alexander that he found himself face to face with a man who, because of his knowledge of and lengthy experience in the country, could help bring his plans for Nova Scotia to a fruitful conclusion. This Huguenot merchant, much neglected by his own country and sympathetic by way of his religion to the Protestant English, saw a new possibility of improving his fortunes on the western side of the Atlantic.

As fate would have it, while in England La Tour fell in love with one of the English Queen's ladies-in-waiting who happened to be related to Alexander. The Frenchman, tired of suffering the neglect of his own countrymen and given the offer of a Nova Scotia knighthood to go along with his new English bride, decided to throw his lot in with the Scotsman. La Tour was probably the first person to suggest to the senior Alexander that he should locate his settlement in the appealing setting of Port Royal.

On May 24, 1629, a somewhat relieved but naturally anxious Alexander bid goodbye to his eldest son who, with a new contingent of settlers and needed supplies, set out for Port Royal. He was accompanied by James Stewart, Lord Ochiltree, who had taken over responsibility for New Galloway in Cape Breton from Sir Robert Gordon. Having fallen upon hard times, as had many in Scotland at the time, he decided to try his luck across the ocean. He raised £500 and gathered together about 60 settlers, many of them English, with whom he hoped to renew his fortune in the new world. The ships carrying the settlers and supplies were part of a larger fleet involving the Kirkes, who were now determined to take Québec.

After safely dodging icebergs and sailing through thick fog, towards the end of a voyage of less than four weeks they sighted Newfoundland. Here the Kirkes, who set sail about the same time, went their own way up the St. Lawrence to confront Champlain and, with his defeat, give England total and unopposed dominion over the young Canada, at least temporarily.

Lord Alexander picked up the surviving members of the group he had left provisioned the previous summer. Many, however, had not lived to see his return: up to 30 of them had died over the winter. Some, inadequately clothed and sheltered against the harsh elements, had succumbed quietly to the bitter cold. Others had experienced the horrors of scurvy. Lacking sufficient fresh food and trying to survive on a diet detrimental to their recovery, their joints swelled, their bodies broke out in sores, and their teeth and hair fell away. These unfortunates died pitifully slow and painful deaths.

Resting briefly after their trans-Atlantic crossing and attending to the needs of the weakened survivors of the previous year, the Alexander party remained on the south coast of Newfoundland for over a week. The enlarged expedition then took to sea again and arrived off the coast of Cape Breton in early July. Ochiltree and his group of colonists disembarked at the old whaling station of Port aux Balienes near present-day Louisbourg, where a small fortification was built. Unfortunately, this was soon taken and destroyed by a French naval force, and the desperate Ochiltree and some of his distraught settlers were shipped back to France as prisoners. After rotting in a French dungeon for over a year and watching some of his fellow prisoners die from their deprivations, he was released, only to end up in an English prison for another seventeen years on a charge of inciting political unrest.

Having dropped off Ochiltree and his charges, Lord Alexander departed on July 14th to complete the final leg of the long voyage.

After passing Canso, the ships skirted down along the south coast of Nova Scotia. It took fourteen days to reach the much-sought-for opening into the Annapolis Basin, which they reached on July 28, 1629, That night, in the golden glow of a mid-summer sunset, the relieved, excited, and ever-hopeful passengers sailed safely on the rising tide into the calm waters of the bay and glimpsed for the first time the serene and fertile surroundings in which they were destined to make their new home.

After spending one or two days exploring the lower reaches of the attractive basin, they sailed upriver. Then, having passed by Goat Island and the ruins of two mainland forts, the former Habitation and a later construction of La Tour's, they chose a site that Alexander's poet friend Drummond later described as "fortified by nature, by sea and by land, rising in ascent on the main river, having on the east of it running a small river." Here they went ashore and planted the new flag. Nova Scotia had been born.

Soon after landing, the men, women, and children gathered together in common prayer under the open sky to give thanks for their safe arrival and to ask a blessing on the enterprise just begun. Then Lord Alexander, with as much solemnity as the small community could muster, officially named the settlement Charlesfort in honour of his sovereign.

The settlers needed to move quickly to protect themselves against the possibility of attack by the French. There were other dangers as well. The thick forests were dark and mysterious and one could quickly get lost in them or become easy prey for whatever wild animals lurked there. There was uncertainty about the Indians. Would the native Mi'kmaq be friendly? Would the dreaded Iroquois appear? The men quickly took to cutting down trees for logs and serious digging was undertaken for the palisaded outer walls, behind which they could mount their small cannons, construct their first shelters, and safely rest.

Nearby were the wheat fields that had been cleared and planted by the former French settlers. The land, although neglected since Poutrincourt's time, responded readily to the new arrivals' first enthusiastic digging and seeding. Whatever it would produce by fall would help keep them healthy through the long hard months of winter. Most had heard about, and some had experienced, the terrors of a Canadian winter and the terrible results of scurvy.

Trade also was to be developed, and efforts were taken to acquire furs. Fortunately for the settlers, the local Mi'kmaq appeared of their own volition and, with the exchange of gifts, friendly relations were quickly established. The dress and lifestyle of the native population were naturally of much interest to the new settlers, who noted that their long black hair was cut short over their foreheads "after the fashion of the Court of England." It can be assumed that the Mi'kmaq, who had already traded with the French, were somewhat less surprised than the new arrivals. Their expertise at hunting and their readiness to trade was no doubt much appreciated by the Charlesfort settlers. For the duration of the Charlesfort settlement's existence, cordial relations existed between the two groups, each benefiting from what the other had to offer. One historic consequence of this contact was a visit to London by the Mi'kmaq chieftain, Sagamo Segipt, who with his wife and son accompanied ships returning to England for additional supplies and settlers later that year. Following their arrival at Plymouth, they were entertained at court, where they met with King Charles I, from whom, according to one correspondent of the day, Segipt asked for protection against the French. What these native North Americans thought of their voyage, the landscape and country houses of England, the crowded streets, the contrasting lifestyles, and the imposing structures they saw in London, can only be imagined.

After the departure of the ships for England, Lord Alexander supervised preparations for the coming winter. He had stayed behind to share the challenges and hardships faced by the settlers during their first full year in their new home. Apart from the risks presented by the elements, a surprise attack, or a sudden outbreak of some disease, there was also the danger of internal strife caused by either religious differences or disgruntled individuals within the settlement. After a winter that claimed some of the settlers, new recruits and more supplies arrived, long overdue and so all the more welcome. Among the new arrivals was Sir George Home, with his wife and children.

When word of the success of the trans-Atlantic voyage and the establishment of the settlement at Charlesfort reached London, a royal letter, dated October 17, 1629, authorized the Scottish Privy Council to institute a voluntary contribution to assist some highlanders to emigrate to Nova Scotia, there still being a poor response from Scottish noble families to the call to participate in the venture. Alexander, encouraged by the news from Nova Scotia, negotiated with highland chieftains to allow clan members to populate his settlement, but he needed the support of the Privy Council to raise money to ship them out. Accordingly, a royal letter was issued to the Council:

"As we do very much approve of that course for advancing the said plantation, and for debordering that our kingdom of that race of people, which, in former times, had bred so many troubles there: so since that purpose may very much impart the public good and quiet thereof, We are most willing that you assist the same, by all fair and laudable ways."

The Council, which surely contained some of Alexander's sworn enemies, failed to respond favourably to this royal request. Its intransigence left Alexander no alternative but to go further into debt, especially since he was now involved in acquiring land on the eastern shore of the Firth of Clyde, where he hoped to establish a permanent port for future traffic and trade to and from Nova Scotia. His optimistic expectations for the settlement were taking him into a financial sink-hole from which, even with the King's help, he would never be able to extricate himself.

Captain David Kirke, having captured Québec and, apparently, visiting Charlesfort on his way home, reported back in England that the settlement was in urgent need of supplies. Sir William's desperation grew as he struggled to raise the funds needed to save the lives of his son and others, surviving he knew not how, in Nova Scotia. He petitioned the King again and on November 17th a royal mandate was issued urging the Privy Council in Edinburgh to raise the necessary finances so a ship could be readied and supplies sent out as soon as possible. Again, they dragged their feet.

Correspondence Alexander wrote through January and February of 1630 indicates that he was becoming increasingly concerned about the well-being of his son at Charlesfort. In a pleading letter from London to the influential Earl of Menteith, his paternal anxiety is obvious:

"As for my own particulars, I have no more to write than I wrote formerly, and especially concerning my son's supply, whereupon his safety or ruin doth depend... there is no money to be had here [in London] which makes me as yet doubtfull what I may do from hence."

Unknown to him, nearly half of the settlers died of the dreaded scurvy during the winter of 1629-30. Finally, in May, the newly knighted and married Claude de La Tour returned to his former abode, carrying with him a letter of congratulation to Alexander's son from the King along with instructions to continue with the settlement. The royal letter also urged him to take special care to appoint a suitable deputy during his absence if he decided to return to England.

La Tour, arriving on the southeast coast of Nova Scotia, failed to persuade his own suddenly patriotic son Charles to side with the English, in spite of the offer of a baronetcy and a sizable tract of land. Even an armed attack staged by the infuriated father failed to dislodge his well-fortified offspring. After spending some time at Charlesfort, the elder La Tour retired to a house alongside his son's rugged stronghold at Cape Sable. Like Champlain, his sails had been filled and then deflated by the ever-changing winds of political fortune that blew around the coasts of Nova Scotia. Unlike Champlain, he seems to have ended his days in quiet domesticity, with his high-born but adaptable young wife in his adopted home.

In the fall of 1630, after more than a year at Charlesfort, William Alexander Jr. set sail for England, leaving Sir George Home in charge. Arriving in England around the middle of October, he discovered that rumours of the Crown returning lands in Canada to the French were closer to the mark than he might have expected. The royals of England and France were preparing to bargain over the terms of a new peace accord that had ended two years of hostilities, and caught in the middle were his father's Nova Scotia and the innocent and unsuspecting settlers he had so recently left behind.

By the 1632 Treaty of St.-Germain, New Scotland was handed back to France, along with Québec and Cape Breton. Charles, desperate for funds and wanting to avoid further conflict with France, settled for a payment of 400,000 crowns from France, the outstanding portion of his French wife's dowry. Meanwhile, he maintained to Alexander and other Baronets that he had ceded only the fort at Charlesfort, and not all of New Scotland. Much confusion followed, and Sir William, for once supported by the Scottish Privy Council, did everything he could to persuade his King not to abandon Nova

Scotia and his subjects still living there. In the end, he had to settle for a worthless warrent for £10,000, lands in New England, and empty titles, while the French began to settle the province.

A royal decree was issued ordering the Charlesfort settlers to abandon the site. Some returned to England, others went to Massachusetts, and at least a few remained to live with the Mi'kmaq or marry French women who arrived after the changeover.

In September 1632, Count Isaac de Razilly, a cousin of Richelieu's, established French administrative headquarters and a farming settlement at LaHave. It was not until at least 1636 that Charlesfort was physically taken over by the French under his successor, Charles de Menou D'Aulnay. From then onwards, Charlesfort disappeared from sight and knowledge of its exact whereabouts and the lives of its inhabitants was lost to history.

In spite of this disastrous turn of events, Alexander continued to faithfully serve his King as an elder statesman, even during years of armed rebellion and insurrection in Scotland. Efforts by Charles to help Alexander recuperate his losses, by granting him royalties from the issuing of new coins and publication of the Anglican *Psalms*, only served to estrange him further from his fellow countrymen. Returning to his first love, Alexander edited and re-published his philosophical plays and poems, a task that must have given him some satisfaction and caused him to pause to consider the course his life had taken. His final years were filled with tragedy and torment. In September 1637, his second son, Anthony, an architect who had risen rapidly to become the King's Master of Works and Head of all Masons, died. A few months later, his eldest son and namesake, who had helped establish Charlesfort, died as well. With his Nova Scotia project in apparent ruins and without hope of financial compensation, the ailing and aging Alexander was mercilessly hounded by creditors.

Then, in September 1640, Alexander, the man who dared with his pen to advise and censure kings and whose wise counsel they in turn sought, who struggled to obtain a place in the new world for his fellow countrymen, died impoverished in London while his concerned creditors gathered at his bedside to claim what they could of his estate. He was buried quietly in a family crypt in the High Church in Stirling. Ridiculed and rejected by many, few of his fellow Scotsmen paid him homage. Considered by some an opportunist, by others a traitor, and by many an impractical idealist and a failure, he had followed a dream, and it had cost him and his family dearly. His faithful and long-suffering wife Janet had to apply for and live on a Crown pension in her remaining years.

But Nova Scotia had been born. Alexander's settlers had built homes, laboured on the land, fished the waters, and established trade with other English colonies to the south during the four or more years of Charlesfort's existence. In the summer of 1654, a Puritan force out of Massachusetts, which may have included a few of the displaced settlers from Charlesfort, succeeded in retaking Nova Scotia from the French. But a long, relentless struggle for the territory had just begun, and many years would pass and many lives be lost before it would be over.

Finally, in 1710, the Nova Scotia flag was again raised on the site of Charlesfort, the newly named Annapolis Royal, now the capital of a British colony that, in time would welcome thousands of Scottish settlers to its shores.

13

The Guthry Letter

Lacking any record of the exact location of Charlesfort and having
no information about the daily lives of its inhabitants, most early
Canadian historians summarily concluded that this small, agrarian
settlement had existed near the ruins of the Port Royal Habitation, at
a site traditionally known, since the early-eighteenth century, as the
"Scots Fort." Such a designation was given in 1725 English military
map to what were then the overgrown remains of a former fort in the
area. However, this designation was not based on any existing documentation. The map's cartographer, in the absence of any other
evidence, simply concluded that it must have been where Alexander's settlers had established themselves.

Over the next century, little or no interest was shown in the
matter. The former existence and significance of Charlesfort seemed
to fade rapidly from memory, overtaken by a succession of larger
and well-documented military installations and events, both at Annapolis Royal and elsewhere in the province. After Nova Scotia's
renowned early author and historian, Thomas C. Haliburton, who
lived for a time in Annapolis Royal, made reference to the "Scots
Fort" in his *History of Nova Scotia*, published in 1829, it became
generally accepted as having been Charlesfort's location. There the
matter seemed to rest undisturbed by either interest or dispute for the
next 100 years.

This same site, by this time a pleasant meadow, was championed
by Harriette Taber Richardson of Cambridge, Massachusetts, an
affluent summer resident of the area, who in 1928 enthusiastically
spearheaded efforts that would lead in 1941 to the complete recon-
struction of the Habitation at Port Royal by the Canadian government. Her success in promoting its rebuilding led her to the
well-intentioned task of petitioning for official recognition for what
she sincerely believed was the nearby site of Nova Scotia's first
British settlement. Although Taber Richardson initially based her

1979 Re-enactment of the landing of Scottish settlers

assumption on the references to the "Scots Fort" on the 1725 military map and in Haliburton's history of the province, some surface features of the grass-covered site, such as a stone wall and a three-metre-wide ditch, seemed to settle the issue for her. She set about convincing others, including Col. E.K. Eaton, then the honorary Superintendent of Fort Anne and Port Royal National Historic Parks, that this indeed was where Charlesfort had been, and that it should receive appropriate official recognition.

In spite of Taber Richardson's obvious conviction, it soon became apparent that some uncertainty existed within official circles about the accuracy of her conclusions. Perhaps comments by historian G.P. Insh in a 1930 article about Alexander's settlement in the *Dalhousie Review* had given them reason to pause. He wrote:

"What is the history of the Scots Settlement?... That history it must be confessed is exceedingly obscure. Of the ingenious and persistent efforts made by Sir William Alexander and his royal masters, King James and King Charles, to foster the colonisation of Nova Scotia, many traces have come down to us.... But the incidents of the voyage, the daily life and labour of the Scottish settlers as they tilled the soil or built their log cabins and their fortalice, are known to us only in the dim light of surmise."

The same could well have been said about the location of the settlement.

When official commemoration of the "Scots Fort" site was first considered by Canada's Historic Sites and Monument Board in 1944, it by no means met with immediate approval. The Nova Scotia member of the Board, Professor C.D. Harvey, sought to have any decision deferred. Minutes of several subsequent Board meetings indicate that there was continual doubt and much debate about the proposal.

This may have resulted in part from a tantalizing clue contained in a book entitled *Sir William Alexander: A Biographical Study*, which had been published just a few years earlier by American historian Thomas H. McGrail, who had obviously done some scholarly research. McGrail quoted from extracts of a previously ignored or unknown account of the expedition's arrival and landing in Nova Scotia. The brief and inconclusive account had been written some 300 years earlier by Alexander's close friend and fellow poet, William Drummond of Hawthornden. While carrying out his research among the Hawthornden Manuscripts at the National Library of Scotland, McGrail had come across an undated description of the settlers' arrival in the Annapolis Basin. Although incomplete, it suggested that the site of the Charlesfort settlement was not at the traditionally accepted location then being considered for official recognition. Written in the English of the first half of the seventeenth century, it was, according to McGrail, probably a condensed transcription of a much fuller account told to Drummond by Alexander's son, or by someone else who had been on the voyage. After briefly describing the settlers' departure from England and their arrival in the Annapolis Basin, which was referred to by its French name of Port Royal, it said:

> "As wee sailed up the river some 3 leagues from the entrye is an island stored with faire trees. Sailing higher wee saw two fortes, one of Poutrincourts another of la Tour disliking both wee advanced to a place fortified by nature toward the sea and land."

Brief and inconclusive as this reference was, it nonetheless indicated that the settlers chose a site farther up the Annapolis River from the remnants of both the original Habitation and another nearby fort, presumably built some years after the Argall raid of 1614, by the La Tours and other former members of Poutrincourt's settlement who remained behind after the Habitation was abandoned.

In spite of this suggestion, McGrail, like other historians before him, linked Charlesfort to the "Scots Fort" site, there being no concrete evidence to indicate otherwise. Perhaps he did not want to question his fellow Canadian academics or appear out of step with accepted historical opinion. Nonetheless, his quote from Drummond underlined two important points: that a second fort, only previously hinted at in other sources, had definitely been built near the original Habitation; and that the Alexander settlers had bypassed the remnants of both in favour of another site farther up the Annapolis River. This should have called into question earlier conclusions about the "Scots Fort" site and led to calls for a more precise and thorough investigation before any official designation was made.

But, although no proper excavation or even an aerial survey had been carried out, and in spite of the lack of even the smallest piece of archaeological evidence, the Historic Sites and Monument Board at its May 1951 meeting unanimously recommended that the suggested site be duly recognized as that of Charlesfort. Perhaps some members of the Board acted out of sympathy for Taber Richardson, whose long illness resulted in her death that same year, or they may have succumbed to political pressure to bring to a conclusion a matter few people knew or cared about. The following year, a cairn containing a bronze plaque commemorating Charlesfort and its illustrious founder was erected on the site and ceremoniously unveiled. The whole matter seemed to have finally been put to rest.

However, some doubts lingered, and concern about the location was again raised at a 1958 meeting of the Historic Sites and Monuments Board. The inference of the Drummond quote would not go away, and McGrail's book remained in print as a haunting reminder that a wrong decision may have been made. But the Board once more danced around the thorny issue, setting it aside for further study. The by-now-embarrassing matter was again diplomatically deferred in 1959 and was quietly forgotten. The Charlesfort question seemed destined to remain an unsolved mystery in the annals of Canadian history.

Then, in 1967, Norah Story, the former Head of the Manuscript Division at the National Archives in Ottawa, wrote in *The Oxford Companion to Canadian History and Literature* that Charlesfort had existed some six miles away from Port Royal and the site officially designated by the Historic Sites and Monuments Board. Unfortunately, Story did not disclose her source (it may have been the same as McGrail's) or indicate exactly where she thought the settlement had been located. Her assertion caused few ripples, and no other voices were raised in opposition to the officially sanctioned site.

Meanwhile, tourists and history buffs flocking to the rebuilt Habitation sometimes visited and photographed the stone cairn commemorating Alexander's settlement at the "Scots Fort," but little publicity was given in tourism promotions to the Charlesfort story. Then, in 1988, a centuries-old letter was accidentally discovered in Scotland that brought the historic 1629 voyage of Alexander's settlers, the location of Charlesfort, and the exciting early days of the settlement dramatically to life. A year later, an archaeological dig in the heart of Annapolis Royal began to produce visible and tangible proof of just where Charlesfort had actually been located.

This letter, as mentioned earlier, had been discovered in Edinburgh by Carleton University Professor Naomi Griffiths. It is a full-length transcript of an official letter entitled *A Relation of the Voyage and Plantation of the Scots Colony in New Scotland under the conduct of Sir William Alexander Younger, 1629,* written by Richard Guthry, one of the Charlesfort settlers, in late August of 1629. Beginning with a detailed and dramatic account of the perilous voyage from England, the Guthry letter provides insight into the variety of people who embarked on this adventure to a new life across the Atlantic and contains many marvellous observations of the nature of the new land the settlers had arrived in and the appearance and customs of the Mi'kmaq.

On returning to Canada, Griffiths brought her accidental find to the attention of a colleague, Professor G. Reid of Saint Mary's University in Halifax. Reid, who teaches early Nova Scotia history, is author of several books on the subject. He was naturally intrigued by the Guthry document and quickly realized that it indicated Charlesfort had been elsewhere than previously thought.

It was obvious from the title of the original thirteen-page document that this was an authorized, contemporary account of this first attempt to establish a British settlement in Nova Scotia. Although it had been proposed and promoted by a Scot and many Scots were among the settlers, it was not entirely a Scottish enterprise. It had been made possible by the approval and support of two successive kings of England, and Englishmen were involved in the voyage as well. Although the full political amalgamation of England and Scotland did not take place until the next century, the word "British" was already in use to denote the associations and interactions between the two countries. In fact, the word was used at least once by the letter's author, suggesting he was acquainted with political currents of the time. The official nature of the correspondence, written in period English, is again quite apparent in the formal opening paragraph, which also suggests that it was intended for Sir William Alexander himself

> "It pleased your honour at my depairtur from England to lay a charge upon me to writt a particular relation of our Voyage at Sea and of the nature and condition both of people and Country where now by the mercy of God we are planted."

The letter then takes the form of a very factual account, interspersed with Guthry's colourful commentary and interesting observations, of the departure from England, the trans-Atlantic voyage, and the arrival of the settlers in Nova Scotia. The occasional use of Scottish and Latin words suggests that Guthry was an educated northerner and, as shall be seen, possibly a minister or doctor.

Richard Guthry began his journal just as the settlers were setting sail in the light of the rising sun on the morning of "Whitsonday," May 24, 1629, having left from "the Dounes." The Downs is an area of shoreline sea north of Dover on the east coast of Kent. The two or three small ships soon reached the English Channel and proceeded westward, helped by a fair wind. Two days later, they encountered the first disturbing experience of the voyage. England and Spain and their respective allies were at war with one another, and the recently announced peace with the old enemy, France, was a fragile one, making the Channel a dangerous place for shipping. To their dismay, the Charlesfort settlers found themselves threatened by a Dutch fleet that mistook them for pirates or hostile privateers. Expecting the worst, the desperate landlubbers "prepared for a fight, but found our suspected enemies disdainful friends, for they gave us a shot ore tuo." Shaken by the experience, but obviously relieved, the party passed out of the Channel into the open Atlantic unhindered by sandbars or sickness, "ore tempest of weather, ore any danger ore hurt from the enemy."

On the 27th, one of the women among the settlers accompanying Lord Ochiltree, perhaps having suffered injury during the frightening encounter with the Dutch fleet, gave birth to a stillborn baby. If this sad event was interpreted by any aboard as an ill omen, Guthry chose to make no comment on the matter. The next notable incident occurred four days later, when keen eyes spotted a sail on the western horizon. As the ships drew close, the settlers were relieved to find an English vessel on its way back to Dover. Its skipper was proudly hauling home a captured Spanish caravel loaded with sugar and tobacco. No doubt this maritime meeting gave the travellers cause to celebrate an English seaman's good fortune and lifted their spirits.

Nothing is then reported for another two weeks, suggesting that the interim period was uneventful, as weeks at sea often are. Then, on June 14th, when they were somewhere southwest of Greenland, they sighted large ice flows or, as Guthry described it, they "espyed sundry great islands of yce at sea."

As disturbing as this must have been to those aboard the small ships, the cold and frightened travellers found themselves facing an even greater threat of imminent disaster early on the morning of the 19th, when they woke to find themselves enveloped in thick fog. Suddenly, they were alarmed to see through the fog an iceberg looming down on them. They managed to avoid a collision with this "great rocke of yce." Later the same day, after the fog lifted, they shared the joy of sighting the welcome coast of Newfoundland, where they "did bear up Southward to St. John's harbour where we anchored all night."

Relieved at their safe arrival, Guthry, an obviously religious man among people who prayed day and night for their safety on the ever-treacherous North Atlantic, readily acknowledged that, like the Israelites' successful crossing of the Red Sea over 2,000 years earlier, Divine intervention had played a hand in "conducting them through the deeps." The ships remained in Newfoundland for about a week, enjoying a much-appreciated rest after their nearly four weeks at sea. Getting his first close-up look at the new world, Guthry appreciatively noted that St. John's Harbour was "a faire entry capable of many ships, where once entered, they are secured because of high mountains breaking the force of the wind on all sids." What Guthry saw of Newfoundland did not, however, impress him. Its geography and climate led him to remark critically that "the land... being bare, rockey, montaneous, and in respect of long bitter winters be almost inhabitable fitter for beasts than men."

Guthry had quite likely learned by then of the horrible deaths from scurvy suffered by many of the earlier settlers and of the intention of Lord Baltimore, who had built a large house and established a fishing settlement at Ferryland on the Avalon Peninsula, to move much farther south to warmer climes in what would later become the American colony of Maryland. Yet Guthry, who may have been a naturalist and an apothycarist, professions much valued in early settlements, carefully noted that, in spite of the harsh conditions in Newfoundland, "there is found some good medicinable hearbs as Salsaparilla, Alisander Angelica, berries of some different kinds, wild fitches." Guthry goes on to bemoan the fact that the lack of any natural cure for scurvy on the island had dire consequences for some of those who had overwintered from the voyage of the previous year, "which makes me with grief and sorrow to relate the pitiful death of many of our young men, that died thereof."

The deaths of so many must have been quite a blow to the younger Alexander, who was counting on their help in establishing the settlement in Nova Scotia. Here Guthry mentions something that suggests he was a cleric. In St. John's he baptized a two-year-old boy named John, perhaps the child of one of the earlier settlers on the island. He then proceeds with his account of the remainder of the voyage, confirming facts already known from other sources and adding some more of his own.

After taking on fresh water and whatever supplies might have been available, the colonists sailed to the southwest. On July 1st they sighted Cape Breton, where they encountered several fishing boats. At English Harbour, which in spite of its name would become the site of the French stronghold of Louisbourg less than 100 years later, they approached one of these boats, but the fishermen, perhaps fearing attack by one of the many pirates who frequented these waters or that they might be pressed into service on an enemy ship, quickly headed for shore and disappeared into the woods. They had better luck about ten kilometres up the coast at another inlet known as Port aux Baleines, where they came across two fishing boats. One was French, out of the port of La Rochelle, whose crews were, according to Guthry, "of the religion," meaning of course that they were Huguenots or Protestants. The other, a Basque vessel, was quickly captured. It was here that Alexander's friend and associate, Lord

Ochiltree, decided to begin his settlement. On the advice of a Captain Ogilvy and with the help of the entire party, he immediately built a small fortification, which he called Rosemarine, on strategic high ground close to the shore. Unfortunately for those who remained with Ochiltree, the Cape Breton settlement, in spite of the peace with France, would be captured and destroyed just a few short weeks later by a French force from Dieppe.

However, Ochiltree had more immediate, internal troubles to contend with, in the form of religious dissent among his settlers. Conflicts among various religious sects had been spreading in Britain for some time, and the hope of many of those who sailed for the new world was that they would finally be free of the resulting strife. From Guthry we learn that, like some terrible disease transferred across the Atlantic by ships' rats, the problem of religious intolerance that had plagued England and Europe for well over a century was also carried onto the new continent

No sooner were members of the Ochiltree plantation ashore when, to everyone else's surprise, a group of extremists suddenly surfaced and took themselves apart from the others, whom they self-righteously considered to be less pure. From the tone of Guthry's comments there is little doubt that this was totally unexpected, and must have have been the cause of much concern:

> "Eight households of his company… shewing there ingratitude to my Lord… refused to joyne stocks with my Lord, and did seperat themselves from their company.They will admit none to their society without publick confession, they will allow no pastorall function… They hold all papists damned and are ray-lors against superiors, refractory to powers especially to Bishops and… England's church."

In a final exasperated comment at the separatist antics of these people whom he referred to as "factionists and schismaticks," the Anglican Guthry exclaimed "good Lord deliver all plantations from such people, and root them out, or convert them where they live."

Guthry seems to have regained his equilibrium by the following Sunday, when he calmly recorded that a regular service of prayers and psalms was held among the remaining settlers. Then, on July 9th, the rocky shoreline became the backdrop for the happy occasion of a wedding of two of the settlers.

Small cannon at Port Royal

Leaving Cape Breton on the morning of the 14th, he and the other members of Sir William Alexander's expedition sailed down the southeast coast of Nova Scotia. After another two weeks at sea, during which time they skirted around Cape Sable and St. Mary's Bay, Guthry's ship anchored in the Bay of Fundy at the entrance to the Annapolis Basin on the afternoon of the 28th. Along the way, they had lost sight of the other ships in the expedition, due to storms and heavy coastal fog. That evening, as his ship slipped gingerly through the narrow shoreline gap on the high tide and entered the wide and attractive basin, Guthry got his first glimpse of their long-awaited and much-anticipated final destination. In words even more profuse and laudatory than those penned by Champlain and Lescarbot, who first viewed the area 25 years earlier, Guthry sang the praises of the large, natural harbour, the idyllic setting, and the abundance and beauty of the surroundings. Alexander, as he eagerly read this glowing description back in London, must have been elated after all his pains at finding that his son and the settlers had arrived in such a well-protected and promising haven:

"Weel may it be termed Port Royall, a royal entrie, a river navigable twenty leagues by ships of the burden of tuo or three hundereth tunns, fortifyed on both sids with hills... and fruitfull

First grinding stone in Canada

vallies adorned and enriched with trees of all sorts, as goodly oaks, high firres, tale beich, and birch of incredible bignes, plain trees, Elme, the woods are full of laurall store of ewe, and great variety of fruit trees, chestnuts, pears, apples, cherries, plumes, and all other fruits."

Guthry then related that the expedition sailed up the basin past Goat Island, which he mentioned as being "three leagues from the entry... a pretty island full of brave timber trees." Beyond were the ruins of two French forts, "the one built by Monsieur PoutrinCourt who was driven out by Sir Samuel Argall ane English Captane... another built by Monsieur Latour."

Here Guthry leaves no doubt that the settlers sailed on to where the Annapolis and Allain Rivers meet, and that they established the settlement of Charlesfort on the high ground above the confluence of the two rivers, the site of present-day Annapolis Royal:

"And disliking both we Sailed higher, and found a place forti-fied by nature, by sea and by land, rising in ascent one the maine river, having on the east of it runing a small river portable for shipps of 300 tunns a league up."

The discovery of the sturdy water mill "built by the Frenshe" confirms that, although it was erroneously described as running to the east, the river was definitely the Allain, which runs a zig-zag course from its source to the south and on the banks of which Poutrincourt had ordered the construction of the mill some twenty years earlier.

Once some of the cargo had been unloaded, the young Alexander moved quickly to put down roots and observe the appropriate formalities, as we learn from Guthry's poignant account of the first formal religious service held in the embryonic surroundings of the settlement: "The first of August the preacher being called by our Generall in nomine Sanctae et individuae trinitatis, was the foundation of the fort laid." The next day saw an encouraging sermon "out of Luke" that ended "with prayers, psalmes and much joy, because the Lord had brought us through the seas, and given us our lott in a pleasant land long looked for by us."

Guthry provides us with details of the design and construction of the walls surrounding Charlesfort which, as might be expected, were intended to provide protection from possible attack. At the same time, at least one and possibly other buildings were begun:

"The platt of the fort wes drawn by Captane Ogilvie in forme of a pentagonon, with many horne works good both for offence and defence... befor the latter end of the month the fort with infinit pains and alacrity both of sea and land men was finished, eight pieces of ordinance plainted, four demie culvering, and four minion, out magasene built and stored, the Generals house formed."

Once settled ashore, the enthusiastic Guthry discovered more evidence of nature's diversity and abundance in the area:

"Goose berries of the collour of ripe grapes, Rose berries, and infinit store yet unknowen by us. And in the woods deere of infinit bignes, as may appear by there heads, besides other beasts apparralled with rich furre... Most sweet and pleasant midowes yeelding variety of flowers and hearbs. Roses of most fragrant smell, Tuleps of diverse kinds... hearbs in aboundance, and those very medicinable."

His learning and knowledge of "apothecaria and aromaticks" comes to the fore again as he names in Latin the numerous wild plants his keen eye spots growing among the grasses and along the banks of the rivers. His concern with finding a natural cure for the dreaded scurvy, which he knew would appear among them during the coming winter, is relieved by his discovery of "Acetosa Marina which must serve for scurvy grasse, also store of scurvy leaf, which must serve for baths."

From the above it is obvious that the settlers depended to a great deal on the benefits, medicinal and culinary, of many wild plants and that their ultimate survival depended to a large extent on what their natural surroundings could provide. Like many other early settlers in North America, they knew they must make every effort to support themselves from the earth, for nutritional as well as economic and practical reasons. An almost child-like wonder at the incredible fertility of the land is evident in Guthry's account of his work on the land alongside the others during the early days and weeks of the settlement:

"The land is most fertile: for I myself dige and hedge a garden platt of sixty foot in length and thirty in breed, and sowed onions, cabbage, turneps, carrets, sorrell, parsneps, radishe, pise, and some barley, to make a tryall, and to our admiration we had them above the ground, some in tuo, some in three, some in four dayes, though it was a dry Season, not having rained a moneth, and being the latter end of Agust, so that by Gods grace we expect a rich crope of whatsoever we trust to the earth."

Adding to the settlers' good fortune was the wide variety of fish and game that filled the nearby waters and woods. Guthry's description must have been read with mouth-watering appreciation by his Scottish master:

"Some small rivers and brooks fall into the great river, all full of divers kinds of fishes; some unknowen by us. We eat lobsters as bige as little children, plenty of salmons and salmon trouts, birds of strange and diverse kinds, haukes of all sorts, doves, turtles, pheasents, partridges, blacke birds, a kind also of hens, wild turkeys, crannes, herones, infinit store of geese and three or four kinds of ducks, Snyps, Cormorants and many sea fouls, whales, seales, castors, otters."

The discovery that nature had such riches in store for them must certainly have convinced everyone in the party that they had indeed found an ideal place to build new homes and start new lives. Like Poutrincourt before him, Alexander planned on a settlement that, as well as generating income from fur-trading, fishing, and mining, would become as self-sufficient as possible.

If they were to develop a trading post at Charlesfort, the settlers needed to make contact with the Indians, but there were none in sight, though it is almost certain that their arrival had been observed and their landing and movements carefully watched by numerous hidden eyes. They had been on the ground ten days before they got their first sight of the Mi'kmaq, when a canoe was suddenly seen swiftly approaching the fortification, its two male occupants briskly pad-dling with oars that, to Guthry's surprise, resembled the flat oven shovels used by bakers. He gives what may have been the first description in English of a Mi'kmaq canoe of the time: "the ribbs of it of small firre knit in with wicker, curiously wrought, and lyned with the barke of trees." The Mi'kmaq brought their households with them: "wifs and children... a few kettles, dishes of rynds of trees, plenty of dogges." The dogs, used mostly for hunting, were likely to end up being eaten in hard times.

To everyone's relief, this initial face-to-face meeting between the native population of Nova Scotia and its first British settlers was a friendly one. Guthry himself was greatly impressed by the encoun-ter and by their appearance:

> "Fair cariaged a people among whom people may live verry well... Naked people with mantles, either of beaver, blanket or deere leather curiously wrought, tyed over there left shoulder with a poynt, without Shirts, with clouts covering their secret parts... comely and personable bodies... long blacke hair... very healthfull, neither blacke nor tanny but swarthish, caused of creasie ointments, wherwith daily they anoint themselves."

Over the following days and weeks, Guthry seems to have ac-quired some knowledge of the Mi'kmaq language and lifestyle, and in this first known letter between Nova Scotia and England we get a rare account of some of the customs and behaviour of the Mi'kmaq, and also an indication of earlier contact with Europeans:

"There language not copious, long words, marred with the Basques language... At the first beginning they beginne by giving gifts which they call Garramercies, and yet expecting gifts again... they will come with garramercies, knowing they shall have meat, drink and other necessaries... [They enjoy] feasting when they meet, till all there store be gone so every day serves itselfe.There habitation is under a tree, covering themselves with boughes and rynds of trees... infinitly loving to there wyves and children, and one to another... great mourners for there dead, some times ten dayes... subtill in their truckings, and nimble fingered."

On August 15th, Charlesfort was visited by a group of Indian men and boys who had sailed across the Bay of Fundy from the Saint John River area. Although Guthry does not say so, they were probably Maliseets, who were already much used to interaction with trans-Atlantic traders. After the customary exchange of gifts, the young Alexander entertained them aboard one of the ships, and a mutually beneficial trading relationship was begun. Still another group of Indians showed up at the end of the month, and their visit introduced the church-going settlers for the first time to an aspect of native spirituality. Among the group was a shaman, described by Guthry as "a consulter with the divell." Strangely enough, this was the only Indian Guthry noticed who sported a beard, suggesting that somewhere in his family background was a European trader or fisherman.

On August 20, 1629 the settlement was solemnly and formally named and, by a happy coincidence, the second of two ships that had gone astray in the coastal fog finally showed up. Lord William Alexander, "with many shott of ordinance, and great joy and solemnity, named the fort King Charles."

Having completed his literary commission, the dutiful Guthry concluded his report to Sir William in words highly expressive of his optimism and faith:

"All of our Company praised be God are in good health and have so continued since there coming from England. We are about our husbandry, digging the ground for corne, which will yeelde it plentifully, as all store of fruits whatsoever; Thus humbly taking my leave, recommending your honour and elect lady with your hopefull offspring to the protection of the Almightie I rest."

Using the French name for the area in which they settled, he respectfully signed off: "ffrom Charles fort in port Royall in New Scotland, the 13 day of Agust an: dom: 1629. Your honours dayly remembrancer in my prayers to the Almightie," and signed his name, "Richard Guthry."

Either Guthry or a later transcriber wrote the wrong date at the end of the letter, since the correspondence had already referred to events that happened on the 20th of the same month and even later. The date of completion of the letter must have been either the 23rd or the 31st.

This error aside, the letter provides a correct chronological and highly informative narrative of the progress of the historic voyage and the arrival of the first group of Nova Scotians on these shores. Reading slowly through it in the quiet confines of the Scottish Record Office in Edinburgh in early 1996, I knew it accurately described the terrain Guthry encountered in the Annapolis Basin area some 367 years earlier. Having myself stood atop the high ground at the junction of the Annapolis and Allain Rivers and taken in the inviting vista of marsh, meadow, and mountain around me, I also knew that Guthry's letter left no doubt as to where Charlesfort had been located.

But Richard Guthry's document, however informative it was about the earliest attempt at British settlement in Nova Scotia, was not of itself sufficient to solve finally the mystery of Alexander's "lost colony." Some tangible proof was also needed. Here providence would again play its timely part.

14

The Evidence Uncovered

Naomi Griffiths' fortunate find of the Guthry letter in Edinburgh occurred just as, thousands of kilometres away back here in Nova Scotia, preparations were being made by staff at the regional office of Canadian Heritage for an archaeological dig at Fort Anne National Historic Site in Annapolis Royal. Its purpose was to confirm the existence of the first known fort on the site, which recorded history maintained was built there by the French around 1636. The project, under the direction of Birgitta Wallace Ferguson, began in the early summer of 1989.

John Reid of Saint Mary's University brought the pertinent contents of the Guthry document to the attention of Brenda Dunn, a historian with Canadian Heritage. She passed on the information to

Birgitta Wallace Ferguson, archaeologist

Wallace Ferguson, who was already actively digging on the western perimeter of Fort Anne.

Featuring restored eighteenth-century British officers' quarters surrounded by well-preserved, earthwork fortifications, Fort Anne was known to have been occupied by a series of earlier fortifications. With a team of up to twenty people, some of them archaeological students, Wallace Ferguson was endeavouring to uncover tangible evidence of the presence of the earliest known French fortification built there. This fort had been under the command of Charles de Menou D'Aulnay, who was appointed Lieutenant-General of Acadie by King Louis XIII after the untimely death of D'Aulney's predecessor, Isaac de Razilly.

De Razilly was a competent and experienced military commander and also a member of the Knights of Malta, an offshoot of the Knights Templars. He had been promptly sent over from France after the 1632 signing of the treaty that returned the region to France, and took command of a sizable expedition that included soldiers, settlers, and priests. In spite of being duly authorized by the King and his own powerful cousin, Cardinal Richelieu, to reoccupy Port Royal and take over Charlesfort, de Razilly chose instead to set up his headquarters at LaHave on Nova Scotia's south shore. After his death, the more aggressive and less diplomatic D'Aulnay reasserted the French presence in Port Royal on the site that later became Fort Anne in Annapolis Royal. Nova Scotian and Canadian histories

The Canadian Heritage dig

recorded his 1636 construction there as being the first fortified settlement on the site. It was hoped that the Canadian Heritage dig
below Fort Anne would produce some artifacts from that period.

Swedish-born Wallace Ferguson was no stranger to unearthing
evidence of early inhabitants on Canada's east coast. She had first
come to Canada in the 1960s as an eager member of the archaeological team involved in the excavation of the Viking settlement at
L'Anse aux Meadows, on the wind-blown and barren northern tip of
Newfoundland. Thirty years later, on an early summer day in 1989,
as she viewed the site of her dig from atop a grassy mound on the
southern perimeter of Fort Anne, she had no idea that, with the help
of the young team she was now in charge of, she was about to make
another historic discovery. Drawing on her professional knowledge
gleaned from her many years of research and work in the field, along
with a kind of archaeological sixth sense, Wallace Ferguson chose
an area in which to concentrate the dig. Excavation was begun on a
small, sod-covered spot on the southwestern edge of the fort's moat.
She suspected that this site offered the best possibility of exposing
seventeenth-century topography, relatively undamaged, or even untouched, by later construction.

Almost straight away, her good judgment was confirmed. Hardly
believing their eyes, team members hit on an inscribed marker or
gravestone, clearly identifiable as from the D'Aulnay period. Fired
up by this fortunate find, they spent the following weeks and months

Excavation at Fort Anne

painstakingly digging and sifting through the surrounding soil and in other areas of the enclosed site.

As is often the case in archaeological field work, it took several years of careful, methodical labour to accumulate the evidence of earlier occupation that lay below the surface. The tedious and at times unrewarding work of opening up and examining ever deeper levels continued over the next four summers. Trenches were sensitively dug, their exposed earthen walls minutely examined, and rivers of loosened soil delicately combed through for bits and pieces of the everyday lives of some of Nova Scotia's earliest known settlers. By the fall of 1992, the excavation work at Fort Anne had produced not only tangible, artifactual evidence, but also visible, topographical proof that the site had been occupied since the early-seventeenth century. The dig achieved its stated objective of confirming the existence of D'Aulnay's occupation of the site. Apart from exposing details of its construction, it also brought to light evidence of the fort's destruction. This resulted from the successful effort in 1654 to regain Alexander's Nova Scotia for Britain. The attack, authorized by Oliver Cromwell, involved forces from Massachusetts led by Robert Sedgewick. It was just one of many military confrontations between England and France in Canada that only ended with the 1759 showdown on the Plains of Abraham outside Québec.

The endless hours of gentle digging, of probing and scraping the earth with tiny trowels and grapefruit knives, uncovered many pieces of seventeenth-century French ceramic ware. Carefully examined by Canadian Heritage Researcher Denise Hensen, they were found to be various types of ceramic found at French sites in North America during the first half of the seventeenth century. They established beyond any doubt the accuracy of written historical accounts of the existance of D'Aulnay's fort, believed to have been the first construction on the site. However, the lucky find early on in the dig was not the only propitious discovery made by the team. Artifacts of yet another, earlier settlementat were also uncovered at the deepest level of the dig. These pointed to an earlier, non-French occupation of the site.

Meanwhile, in the summer of 1992, John Reid and Naomi Griffiths, having already come to their own conclusions about the authenticity and accuracy of the Guthry letter, published their article about its historical significance in *The William and Mary Quarterly*. By late 1994, Birgitta Wallace Ferguson had analyzed the findings of the four-year dig at Fort Anne and published a report that focussed on the unexpected non-French discoveries she and her team had made. For over a year, only a small circle of archaeologists and historians were aware of the new conclusions contained in these publications. Fortunately, by the time I made my initial research visit to Annapolis Royal and the "Scots Fort" in the fall of 1995, several people in the area were also becoming aware of the new findings.

In the introductory remarks of her report, archaeologist Wallace Ferguson points out that the dig at Fort Anne had uncovered evidence of two early constructions that in some places seemed to overlap. The first unexpected surprise at the D'Aulnay level was the discovery

Weserware pottery artifact discovered at the excavation

of a piece of pottery not commonly found in French-occupied sites of the period. On examining it, researcher Denise Hansen discovered that it was a piece of "weserware," manufactured in Germany between 1590 and 1625, primarily for export to northern Europe and Britain. Weserware had rarely been found on this side of the Atlantic, and then only at sites of early-seventeenth-century British settlements. It had never previously been found at any other French settlement in North America.

Intrigued by this odd find and still preoccupied with the work of uncovering further evidence of the D'Aulnay fortification, Wallace Ferguson heard about the discovery of the Guthry letter with its tantalizing details about the location of Alexander's 1629 settlement. She quickly realized that she and her team might be in the unique and fortunate position of producing factual evidence to give solid

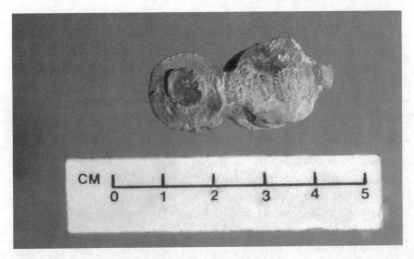

Weserware artifact displaying the Scottish emblem of a thistle

substance to Guthry's letter. As the dig progressed, it became charged with an added sense of expectancy.

During the three remaining summers, other pieces of weserware were uncovered, as was a lead seal, on one side of which there was the distinctively Scottish emblem of a thistle. The seal also sported a seventeenth-century shipping emblem and was, according to Hansen, of a kind used by British cloth manufacturers of the period.

Perhaps even more convincing was the discovery on the perimeter of the site of a palisade. Although only a few segments of its western portion were uncovered, they were enough to indicate that it had been approximately 28 metres in diameter. A bend in one of its segments suggested that the outer wall of the settlement was somewhat irregular in shape, verifying to some degree the description of the fort's design in Guthry's document. The evidence also suggested that the posts that made up the palisade had later been removed to make way for a moat and earthworks. Imprints of wooden sills, ox hooves, and cart wheels were found below the level of the buildings that once stood in D'Aulnay's fort.

The evidence strongly suggested to Wallace Ferguson that D'Aulnay had taken over and added to an existing fortified settlement, and only years later had made changes to the outer walls. In her concluding remarks to her report she states:

"Although the evidence is slender, there is little doubt that the documentary and archaeological evidence prove that the Scots fort was located at what is now the Fort Anne National Historic Site. The archaeological records suggest that the Scots fort was not destroyed but incorporated into the subsequent French fort."

Her conclusion dove-tailed with French documentary material which suggested that Charlesfort had not been destroyed as ordered, but had been occupied by D'Aulney, who, instead of building his own fort, simply modified the existing British one. After reading through the report of the archaeological discoveries, I was convinced that enough solid evidence had been found to finally confirm the true location of Charlesfort.

The implications of both the Guthry document and the Fort Anne archaeological evidence were presented at a conference, which dealt with various cultural and social aspects of early Scottish-Nova Scotian connections, held at Saint Mary's University in September of 1996. After Birgitta Wallace Ferguson's detailed audio-visual presentation, I learned from her that Canadian Heritage had finally decided to relocate the stone cairn and plaque from the "Scots Fort" site beside the Port Royal Habitation to the southwestern perimeter of Fort Anne.

I was also pleased to discover that plans were underway to design and mount in the museum at Fort Anne in the summer of 1997 a detailed, permanent exhibit acknowledging the leading role played by Sir William Alexander in the early history of both Nova Scotia and Canada. Designed and developed by Wayne Kerr of Canadian Heritage, it is also a fitting tribute to the courage and faith of those men and women, who set out across the wide Atlantic, almost 370 years ago, to establish historic Charlesfort.

15

Masons, Mining, and a Mansion

Although the man who gave Nova Scotia its name, flag, coat of arms, and its first English-speaking settlement has now been recognized for these heroic and historic achievements, there remain some related matters that, to my mind, merit mention and further investigation.

During my two years of research for *Oak Island Secrets*, I became increasingly aware that Sir William Alexander might have been associated with or aware of the work which, according to the radio-carbon dating of organic material found on the island, went on there sometime in the sixteenth or seventeenth centuries. Between 1621 and 1632 Alexander enjoyed not only the power and prestige of being a close confidant to two Stewart kings but also possessed the Nova Scotia charter. This gave him regally sanctioned rights to the territory, its riches and resources, its mines and minerals, its coastal waters and surrounding islands. Among the many powers vested in him by the charter was the authority to grant access to others, and to dispose to others any part, large or small, of Nova Scotia.

In the absence of any documentation or other supporting historical evidence, one can only theorize that Alexander knew of a plan to hide and preserve something of great value on Oak Island, but, as I argued in *Oak Island Secrets*, his extensive literary and philosophical interests, his commercial mining activities, his powerful connections at court, and his association with men involved in the then-emerging Masonic movement in Scotland and England all point strongly to that possibility.

While writing this book, I again came across interesting and tantalizing evidence which also points suggests that Alexander was at least indirectly associated with some highly secretive activity here. If true, that activity, which would certainly have had the blessing of the besieged Stewart monarchy, took the form of a secret pursuit of esoteric spiritual studies, the clandestine development of a gold-mining operation, and the building of a secluded but strategically placed mansion on a hillside in the heart of Nova Scotia.

As has become known in recent years, Freemasonry played a prominent part in the lives of some leading figures in the early political and cultural life of the United States. The same is true, although to a lesser extent, in Canada. My research into the history, teachings, and practices of Masonry and Rosicrucianism has shown me the extent to which these organizations had both evolved in Scotland, England, and Europe during the sixteenth and seventeenth centuries and the degree to which their ideals and activities had been brought to North America by some of the people involved with the early colonies.

Originating, according to some, in the Middle East at the time of the building of the great Egyptian pyramid of Giza and incorporating aspects of later European secret societies, Freemasonry first surfaced in its present form in Scotland around 1600, at a time when Europeans were giving serious attention to the new world.

Major Gerald G. Vickers, past Grand Secretary of the Grand Lodge of Nova Scotia, claims that Freemasonry is not a secret society but rather an altruistic, morally uplifting, beneficient society that for centuries has used allegory, symbolism, and ritual to educate and instruct its members. Having carried out extensive independent research into the history and nature of "the Craft," I can only wholeheartedly agree with him.

As a once-powerful organization that has been shrouded in secrecy for centuries, it has naturally had its share of abusers, exploiters, manipulators, and the morally degenerate. It is therefore not surprising that, in spite of its unheralded contributions to society over the years, it has at times been surrounded by enormous controversy and has been repeatedly attacked by uninformed critics.

There is a strong historic tradition in Freemasonry that, during the 200-year period of Crusades into Palestine and the occupation of several Middle Eastern centres by the militantly religious Order of the Knights Templar, some of them became acquainted with the activities and teachings of Eastern mysticism. On returning to Europe, they are believed to have brought this knowledge back with them and incorporated it into their own religious practices. This chivalrous and secretive order became one of the most wealthy organizations in the known world at the time. But by the beginning of

the fourteenth century, the Templars had fallen afoul of the forces of
religious orthodoxy and political ambition in Europe. Templar prior-
ies were suddenly attacked and many members were imprisoned.
Some were ruthlessly tortured and executed in France. In 1307, the
order was disbanded and its surviving members excommunicated
from the Roman church by Pope Clement V. Some Templar knights
were believed to have escaped either west out into the Atlantic or
north to Scotland, with their treasure intact. There is certainly convincing evidence that some made it to Scotland, where they were
given refuge by some of Scotland's noble families. A growing body
of opinion holds that they and their offspring later participated alongside their Scottish cousins and kinsmen in heroic exploits on land
and sea.

Such is part of the background to the alleged voyage of the Earl
of Orkney, Prince Henry Sinclair, who is reputed to have followed
the Viking route across the North Atlantic in the company of other
knights and missionary monks and reached Nova Scotia in 1398.

The Templars, with their enormous wealth, new-found knowledge of Middle Eastern architecture, and their various overlapping
religious influences, infused the masons of the Middle Ages — the
men who built the great cathedrals and castles of Europe — with
their own mythical history. Their visually stunning creations were
testimony to the fact that they or their masters were privy to some
rare knowledge of geometry, mathematics, and symmetric design.
This made the stonemasons of the Middle Ages the *creme de la
creme* of artisans and craftsmen, and gained them both a secure
livelihood and the right to maintain trade secrets within a self-organ-
ized and well-protected trade guild.

In Scotland at the time of Sir William Alexander, we find some
of the earliest evidence of the development of modern Masonry and
of what became known and practiced as Freemasonry in Nova Scotia
and elsewhere in North America.

This shift of emphasis from the purely practical side of the craft
of masonry — known in Masonic historical terms as the Operative-
-to a profoundly philosophical form richly imbued with the concept
of personal transformation — the Speculative or Symbolic — surfaced in Scotland in 1599. William Schaw, General Surveyor, Master
of Works and Chief Architect to James VI, is considered to have been
the man most responsible for this. He began court life as a page to
the Queen Regent around 1560, and through his education and travels

abroad, and his powerful proximity to the royals, attained his important position at court by 1583. The responsibilities of the King's Master of Works, a position later occupied by two of Alexander's sons, included the handling of administrative and financial affairs relating to the building and maintenance of all royal buildings in the realm, as well as the day-to-day design and construction work on numerous projects carried out by stonemasons and related craftsmen.

The Schaw family estate at Sauchie near Stirling was not far from Alexander's in Clackmannan. The families almost certainly knew each other, given their close proximity, shared common interests in literature and philosophy, and connections to court. It is reasonable to assume that Schaw may have introduced Alexander to the practice of Masonry, and his sons to the related profession of architecture

In exploring the life of Sir William Alexander, I found many indications of his participation in that Renaissance-spawned movement which included artists, philosophers, scientists, writers, and others involved in trans-Atlantic adventures that sought to preserve and propagate ancient classical learning while openly promoting and adding to the advancement of human knowledge and experience. Although I could not find any documentation to prove it, I came to the conclusion that Alexander, who was also a profoundly religious man, must have had some association with the esoteric practice of Masonry.

Having been given access to its extensive library by the Grand Lodge of Nova Scotia, I was not surprised to find that there were official records of organized Masonic activity in North America dating back to 1730. However, an unexpected discovery awaited me in the *History of Freemasonry in Nova Scotia*, by noted Halifax lawyer and author Reginald Harris. A past Grand Master and Grand Historian of the Lodge, he states that Freemasonry was probably practiced in the province long before official records were kept. Then to my complete surprise, among the Masonic papers lodged with the Nova Scotia Public Archives, to which I was also given authorized and unlimited access, I came across another Harris publication. This was about Alexander and his colony at Charlesfort. Its contents not only established the Alexander family's connection to the highest levels of Masonry in Scotland and at court but also made the case that the practice of Freemasonry was alive and well in Nova Scotia at the time of Charlesfort.

After arguing that circumstantial evidence seemed to support the often-disputed claim that King James VI was a Mason, Harris cites evidence from records of the day confirming that Sir William Alexander's two eldest sons, William and Anthony, were also inducted as Masons in Edinburgh.

That there were Freemasons active in early Nova Scotia is also suggested by one of the earliest pieces of documentary evidence I came across concerning Masonic activity in North America. According to Frederick Harris, Reginald's father, there is a very rare Masonic publication entitled *Ahiman Rezon* in the library of the Grand Lodge of Massachusetts which contains a concise account of the progress of Freemasonry in Nova Scotia from the days of first European settlement. Harris quotes from this publication in his *History of Freemasonry in Canada*:

"From Europe the Royal Art crossed the Atlantic with the first emigrants and settled in various parts of America. It is said to have been known in Nova Scotia, while in the hands of the French, but however this may be, it is certain that as soon as the English took possession of it they took care to encourage this charitable institution. They saw that it had a tendency to relieve distress and to promote good order."

The reference to the French could well relate to the discovery, late in the nineteenth century, of a large stone near the site of the Habitation, on which were carved the Masonic emblems of a square and compass and the date 1606. Harris then goes on to make some more direct connections among Freemasonry, Charlesfort, and the Alexanders:

"In an interesting paper entitled *First Glimpses of Masonry in North America* read by the late S.D. Nickerson, Grand Secretary, before the Grand Lodge of Massachusetts in March 1891, I find a reference to a tradition among Masonic historians to the effect that Lord Alexander, son of Sir William Alexander, may have been initiated an entered apprentice during his residence in Nova Scotia... C. Murray Lyon in his *History of Freemasonry in Scotland* gives extracts from the original minutes of the Lodge at Edinburgh showing that on the 3rd day of July, 1634 Lord Alexander, son of Sir William, was admitted

Fellow of the Craft in the lodge. No other record of Lord Alexander's Masonic career has been found and it has been accordingly suggested, and it is of course not impossible, that he may have been initiated by some of the brethren whom he found at Annapolis [Charlesfort, Nova Scotia] and was afterwards admitted a fellow of the craft at Edinburgh."

Harris then makes the following interesting point. According to the rules set down by William Schaw in 1598, a member of the Fraternity had first to serve and study at the level of Apprentice for several years before he could be eligible for initiation as a Fellow in Craft, or Master Mason. So, Lord Alexander either was already a Freemason when he arrived in Nova Scotia, where he and others would have continued the practice, or else he was inducted into the Craft for the first time by others during his time at Charlesfort. All this lends credence to the possibility that the study and practice of the craft of Masonry came to Nova Scotia through the efforts of Sir William Alexander.

It is established that Alexander had been involved in mining projects in his native Scotland, that his first such enterprise began in 1607 in Menstrie, and that by 1611 he had also been granted a licence by King James I to refine "silver with quicksilver [mercury] water and salt for twentie ane yeirs." He then embarked on a much larger project at the King's former silver mines at Hilderstone. The ensuing four-year experience taught him much about the trials and tribulations of mining precious metals.

Alexander also had court contacts with others involved in mining. Prominent among them was Thomas Bushell, a former student of Sir Francis Bacon and the King's brilliant young mining engineer. Bushell, who gained a name for himself by extracting ore from flooded shafts, is thought to have visited Nova Scotia, presumably for a mining operation of some kind. Not surprisingly, his name has also been associated with Oak Island.

Sir William's Nova Scotia charter gave him, among other things, the sole right to explore for and extract any minerals he or his agents might find here. It was naturally in his own best interest, and those of the King and the colony, that some effort be made to search out a source of mineral wealth. The fabulously enriching Spanish discoveries in Central and South America had led many later new-world explorers and colonizers to hope they might find even a fraction of such wealth. From the days of Jacques Cartier, we read of efforts made to find gold, silver, or precious stones on the east coast of Canada. Copper and tin were also being sought. In fact, it was just such a search that first brought the French to Port Royal. One must logically assume that, while he had access to Nova Scotia, and particularly while his son, servants, and ships were in these waters, serious attempts were actually made to find some mineral wealth.

One of the standard procedures followed under such circumstances was to carefully scan the shoreline from small coastal vessels for any signs of exposed ore bodies. Another was to examine the estuaries of rivers in the search of evidence of upstream mineral wealth in the riverbed. If such evidence was found, the river was then explored to its headwaters. If Sir William Alexander initiated such efforts in Nova Scotia, they were undertaken without fanfare, and remained well-kept secrets. That would certainly have been the case

The excavation at New Ross

if gold in any quantity was discovered. Alexander's previous mining experience in Scotland, along with his King's urgent need for a new source of wealth to meet his debts and finance his stand against a hostile Parliament, would have meant that any such find would have been shrouded in the strictest secrecy.

There is no documented evidence to suggest that the Gold River, which runs from its headwaters beyond the village of New Ross in central Nova Scotia into the Atlantic just east of Oak Island, was worked by very early settlers, although old stories do persist. Gold was certainly mined there during the last century, and there is some circumstantial evidence to suggest that there was once a refining operation in the area. Some years ago, Dr. Bruce Keddy and Professor Lloyd Dickie carried out an archaeological dig on the site of some alleged ruins of a 300-year-old mansion in the hillside village of New Ross. From my many conversations with them, I learned that laboratory tests conducted on samples of sand collected at the site indicate it contained high levels of gold dust. One conclusion that might be drawn from this, and one that Dickie agrees with, is that the dust may have accumulated as a result of a refining operation there. The previous owner of the site, Joan Harris, had discovered and excavated what she believed were stone foundations of an old building under the sod of her back garden, and a combination of intuitive perception, guesswork, and historical research led her to believe that the foundation walls once supported a seventeenth-century mansion. She also suggested that Vikings had once occupied the site. She found a variety of artifacts buried in the soil, including arrowheads, handmade nails, a piece of a very old sword, and several wooden, shuttle-like objects bound at one end with gut. An archaeologist visiting the site told her that the latter devices resembled tools once used by goldsmiths. I recalled that one of Alexander's mining partners back in Scotland had been Edinburgh goldsmith Thomas Foullis.

None of this, of course, proves that there ever was a mansion or a gold-refining operation in New Ross during the early-seventeenth century. Though the theory that Alexander may have been associated with such an operation is very speculative, there is, I believe, enough reason to further explore the possibility, especially when one takes into account the timing of some of the work done at Oak Island and the indisputable fact, based on hard evidence, that a building once stood on the New Ross site and that people with extensive knowledge of early mining techniques and with some understanding of esoteric

symbolism, Masonic or otherwise, are known to have been se-
cretively active in the Mahone Bay area.

I visited New Ross several times in 1992 and 1993 while doing
research for my book on Oak Island. I was naturally curious to see
the lie of the land where I had heard that a "castle" had existed
centuries earlier. There were also stories that Phoenicians from North
Africa, the adventurous Vikings, or the sea-faring Prince Henry
Sinclair might have been responsible for a settlement of some kind
there. Given the discovery of the Viking settlement in Newfoundland, I felt that nothing could be discounted.

Joan and Ron Harris had moved away, and the property was
vacant and for sale. In view of the many stories associated with the
property, including sensational and unsubstantiated claims made by
Michael Bradley in his book *Holy Grail Across the Atlantic*, I explored the possibility of renting the property for a year, in order to
do some digging of my own and talk to people in the area. But the
house's roadside location was not all that attractive and I felt I would
be too far away from Oak Island, my primary interest at the time.

Following the publication of *Oak Island Secrets*, I had several
lengthy conversations with Keddy and Dickie, the two men who did
some later excavation work on the site near a purported "standing
stone." Their well-photographed dig established the fact that the
upright stone on the property did not mark a well, as has been
recently suggested. Beneath the stone they came across some pieces
of charcoal, the result of either a natural or man-made fire, which
subsequent radio-carbon dating traced back to about 1500 B.C.

Over the last three years, I have had occasion to visit the site and
talk with the present owner, Alva Pye. Like many others, he takes at
face value the now popular theory that Prince Henry Sinclair came
to New Ross and that the alleged foundations of a former building,
which have yet to be investigated by any extensive archaeological
dig, date back to at least medieval times. Over this period, as I
gradually became aware of the confusing array of claims linking
different people and varying purposes to the site and the counter-
claims of cautious government officials and academic historians, I
hoped I might some day meet with the former owners, the Harrises,
to discuss their thoughts and beliefs of the matter. But they had
apparently distanced themselves from, and were remaining noticeably silent about, the whole affair. Then, during a social gathering
last Christmas, Barbara Holzmark, an avid student of Celtic history

and lore, who had spent time with the Harris couple at their New Ross home, gave me a manuscript written by Joan Harris during her twenty years of exploring and researching the land behind her former home. Accompanying notes also contained her critical comments on Bradley's book, which she felt glossed over her findings and conclusions in favour of his own speculations about the New Ross site.

From her manuscript, I discovered that Joan Harris was convinced that the ruins in her back garden were partly the remains of a seventeenth-century mansion built during the reign of either King James I or Charles I as a possible trans-Atlantic refuge for the Stewarts. She also suggests that it had been destroyed in 1654 by Robert Sedgewick's English forces, who descended on Nova Scotia on secret orders of Oliver Cromwell, the avowed enemy of the monarchy and the man primarily responsible for the execution of Charles I. This was conformed in a later phone conversation with her in Ontario. Harris also claims that the renowned Stewart architect, Inigo Jones, had built the mansion for the King, whose headless ghost she also claimed she saw standing on the site.

I remembered that two of Alexander's sons, Lord William and Anthony, had been architects and had successively held the office of the King's Master of Works. They built for the Stewart monarchy and, as the men in charge of all masons in the realm, had a virtual army of tradesmen to call on as needed. Anthony had designed and built an impressive Renaissance manor house for his father in Stirling. Might not he also have been involved in something similiar here in Nova Scotia? It was not impossible, given the availability of skilled manpower and local building materials. After all, the French had built the impressive Habitation in 1605, and Lord Baltimore had a mansion built at Ferryland on the east coast of Newfoundland during the time Alexander held the Nova Scotia charter. The key men in any such construction were likely members of trade guilds, and possibly of the Masonic Order, and, being under the direct authority of the King's Master of Works, they would have sworn to a vow of life-long secrecy.

Although Harris' theory concerning the existence and later destruction of a mansion on her property remains to be proven, her background of Nova Scotia and English history is right on. After capturing the French headquarters established by D'Aulnay at present-day Annapolis Royal, part of Sedgewick's considerable forces likely proceeded to other known French forts, such as those at Cape

Sable and LaHave. This would have brought them within easy reach of Mahone Bay and the Gold River.

Sedgewick's Puritan-driven religious campaign against the Catholic French might well have been extended, as Joan Harris claims, to searching out and destroying the structural remnants of the former Stewart monarchy on a remote but accessible hillside in Nova Scotia. The prospect of getting their hands on some gold would have made the venture even more appealing to Cromwell and the Massachusetts Puritans.

Of course, the references, photos and diagrams in Joan Harris' manuscript fall far short of anything that would normally be considered a seventeenth-century English manor house. But one must remember that the location was far from the centre of power and prestige. Designed, in the tradition of a Scottish keep, more for defence than for comfort, the building would have served several purposes apart from that of accommodation. Since Mahone Bay itself and the mouth of the Gold River were not defensible by seventeenth-century standards and tactics, and, assuming that gold had been found in the vicinity of New Ross, it would have been logical to build a defensible structure on strategic high ground from which any approaching enemy could be observed.

Although this theory does not in any way detract from the possibility that, as Joan Harris claims in her manuscript, the site had been inhabited by others, including the Mi'kmaq and Vikings, much earlier, it leaves me anxious to see a professional archaeological dig carried out to prove whether a seventeenth-century building once stood near New Ross. If one did, it was likely built with Sir William Alexander's knowledge and help. Although much has now been brought to light about the life and times of this remarkable Renaissance Scot and his heroic efforts to establish the historic settlement of Charlesfort, perhaps the full story of the earliest known Scottish link to Nova Scotia has yet to be told.

Bibliography

Acadia University Library: "The Earl of Stirling's Register of Royal Letters Relating to the Affairs of Scotland and Nova Scotia, 1615-1635," Volume I (private) Edinburgh, U.K., 1885.

Alexander, Sir William: *An Encouragement to Colonies*, Da Capo Press and Theatrum Orbis Terrarum, Amsterdam, 1968 (first edition, London, 1624).

Ashe, Geoffrey (Ed.): *The Quest for America*, Praeger Publishers, New York, U.S.A., 1971.

Balfour, Sir James: *The Scots Peerage*, Volume III, Somerville Winton, Edinburgh, U.K., 1911.

Baigent, Michael and Leigh, Richard: *The Temple and the Lodge*, Jonathan Cape, London, U.K., 1989.

Barnard, Murray: *Salt, Sea and Sweat*, Four East Publishing and Nova Scotia Department of Fisheries, Halifax, Nova Scotia, 1986.

Bazain, Germain: *Histoire de L'Art, Mazin*, Paris, France, 1953.

Billings, Malcolm: *The Cross and the Crescent*, BBC Publications, London, U.K., 1987.

Biggar, H. P. (Ed.) *Samuel de Champlain Works*, Volume VI, University of Toronto Press and The Champlain Society, Toronto, Ontario, 1936.

Bothwell Gosse, A.: *The Knights Templar*, London, U.K., 1912.

The British North American Society Annals, Five Volumes: Halifax Regional Municipal Library, Halifax, Nova Scotia.

British Public Records Office: "Calendar of State Papers, Colonial Series," CO 1, 2, 3, 4, 5, 6, 7. "State Papers for Scotland," 14, 15.

Brown, George W. (Ed.): *The Dictionary of Canadian Biography*, *Volume I, 1000-1700*, University of Toronto Press and La Presse de L'Université Laval, Toronto, Ontario, 1966.

Brown, Ivor: *Shakespeare in His Time*, Thomas Nelson and Sons, Edinburgh, U.K., 1960.

Cayce, Edgar Evans: *Mysteries of Atlantis Revisited*, Harper and Row, San Francisco, U.S.A., 1988.

Cell, Gillian T.: *Newfoundland Discovered, 1610-1630*, The Hakluyt Society, London, U.K., 1982.

Charlton, H. B. and Kastner, M. A. (Eds.): *The Poetical Works of Sir William Alexander,* Earl of Stirling, Volumes I and II, William Blackwood and Sons, Edinburgh, U.K., 1921.

Chitnis, Anand C.: *The Scottish Enlightenment*, Croom Helm, London, U.K., 1976.

Christmas, Peter: *Wejkwapnniaq,* Mi'kmaq Association of Cultural Studies, Sydney, Nova Scotia, 1977.

Clement, W. H. P.: *The History of the Dominion of Canada*, William Briggs, Copp, Clark Company, Toronto, Ontario, 1897.

Chute, Marchette: *Shakespeare of London*, E. P. Dutton and Company, New York, U.S.A., 1949.

Costain, Thomas B.: *The White and the Gold*, Doubleday Canada, Toronto, Ontario, 1954.

Davis, Stephen A.: "Micmac," from the "People of the Maritimes" series, Four East Publications, Tantallon, Nova Scotia, 1991.

Dawson, Joan: *The Mapmaker's Eye*, Nimbus Publishing and the Nova Scotia Museum, Halifax, Nova Scotia, 1988.

Dawson, Joan: *Issac de Razilly, 1578-1635*, Lunenburg County Historical Society, Lunenburg, Nova Scotia, 1982.

Dean, Leonard (Ed.): *Renaissance Poetry*, Prentice-Hall, Englewood Cliffs, New Jersey, 1961.

Denys, Nicholas: *Description and Natural History of the Coasts of Nova Scotia*, The Champlain Society, Toronto, Ontario, 1902.

Denys, Nicholas: *Natural History of the People, of the Animals, of the Trees and Plants of North America, and of its Diverse Climates*, (translated by W. F. Ganong) The Champlain Society, Toronto, Ontario, 1908 (first edition, Paris, 1672).

Donaldson, Gordon: *The Scottish Reformation*, Cambridge University Press, Cambridge, U.K., 1960.

Donaldson, Gordon: *Scotland: James V to James VII*, Oliver and Boyd, Edinburgh, U.K., 1965.

Donaldson, Gordon: *The Scots Overseas*, Robert Hale, London, U.K., 1966.

Doughty, Arthur G. and Short, Adam: *Canada and its Provinces*, Brook, Toronto, Ontario, 1914.

Douville, Raymond, and Cassanova, Jacques-Donat: *Daily Life in Early Canada*, The MacMillan Company, New York, U.S.A., 1968.

Dover, K. J. (Ed.): *Ancient Greek Literature*, Oxford University Press, Oxford, U.K., 1980.

Drummond, William:"The Hawthornden Mss.," Ms.2061, etc., The National Library of Scotland, Edinburgh, U.K. c.1635.

Durant, Will and Durant, Ariel: *The Story of Civilization*, Volume VII, The Age of Reason Begins, Simon and Schuster, New York, U.S.A., 1961.

The English Historical Review, Volume XXV: "The Knights Templar in the British Isles," London, U.K., 1910.

Fawcett, Richard: "Argyll's Lodging, Stirling," Historic Scotland, Edinburgh, U.K., 1996.

Ferguson, Bruce and Pope, William: *Glimpses Into Nova Scotia History*, Lancelot Press, Hantsport, Nova Scotia, 1974.

Finnan, Mark: *Oak Island Secrets*, Formac Publishing, Halifax, Nova Scotia, 1995.

Ganong, W. F.: "Crucial Maps in the Early Cartography and Place-Nomenclature of the Atlantic Coast of Canada," The Royal Society of Canada and University of Toronto Press, Toronto, Ontario, 1964.

Grand Lodge F. & A.M. of Pennsylvania: *Freemasonry: A Way of Life*, Philadelphia, U.S.A., 1983.

Grant, Michael: *Latin Literature: An Anthology*, Penguin Books, Middlesex, U.K., 1979.

Gregory, Lady Augusta: *Irish Mythology*, Slaney Press, Dublin, Ireland, 1994.

Griffiths, Naomi E. S. and Reid John G.: "New Evidence on New Scotland, 1629," *The William and Mary Quarterly*, Williamsburg, VA, U.S.A., July, 1992.

Hakluyt, Richard: *Principal Navigations, Traffiques and Discoveries of the English Nation*, Viking Press, New York, U.S.A., 1965.

Haliburton, Thomas C.: *An Historical and Statistical Account of Nova Scotia*, J. Howe, Halifax, Nova Scotia, 1829.

Hannon, Leslie F.: *The Discovers: The Seafaring Men Who First Touched the Coasts of Canada*, McClelland and Stewart, Toronto, Ontario, 1971.

Harris, Frederick W.: *The Beginning of Freemasonry in Canada*, Grand Lodge of Nova Scotia, Halifax, Nova Scotia, 1938.

Harris, Reginald V.: *Sir William Alexander and His Scottish Colony in Nova Scotia*, Grand Lodge of Nova Scotia, Halifax, Nova Scotia, 1954.

Harris, Reginald V. and Longley, Ronald S.: *Freemasonry in Nova Scotia: A Short History*, Grand Lodge of Nova Scotia, Halifax, Nova Scotia, 1966.

Harvey, Daniel C.: "Sir William Alexander and Nova Scotia," Nova Scotia Historical Society Collection, Volume XXX, Halifax, Nova Scotia, 1954.

Henderson, Thomas Finlayson (Ed.): *Dictionary of National Biography*, Volumes III and VI, Stephen-Lee, London, U.K., 1917.

Hosmer, J. K. (Ed.): "A History of New England, 1630-1649," Winthrop's Journal, New York, U.S.A., 1908.

Howarth, Stephen W. R.: *The Knights Templar*, Atheneum Press, London, U.K., 1982.

Howell, James: *Instructions for Forreine Travell*, T. B. for Humprey Mosley, London, 1642.

Insh, George P: *Scottish Colonial Schemes, 1620-1686*, MacLehose Jackson and Co., Glasgow, U.K., 1922.

James VI of Scotland: *Basilicon Doran*, Volumes I and II, Robert Waldergraue, Edinburgh, U.K., 1599.

James VI of Scotland: *Poetical Exercises at Vacant Hours*, Robert Waldergraue, Edinburgh, U.K., 1591.

Johnson, John: *Annapolis Royal and Area*, Historical Association of Annapolis Royal, Annapolis Royal, Nova Scotia, 1908.

Jones, Elizabeth: *Gentlemen and Jesuits*, University of Toronto Press, Toronto, Ontario, 1986.

Kenyon, John P.: *Stuart England*, St. Martin's Press, New York, U.S.A., 1978.

Laurie, William Alexander: *The History of Freemasonry and the Grand Lodge of Scotland*, Grand Lodge of Edinburgh, Edinburgh, U.K., 1850.

Lehane, Brendan: *The Northwest Passage*, Time-Life Books, Alexandria, Va., U.S.A., 1981.

Lescarbot, Marc: *The History of New France*, Volumes I-III, The Champlain Society, Toronto, Ontario, 1907-14 (first edition, Paris, 1609).

Lindsay, Maurice: *History of Scottish Literature*, Robert Hale, London, U.K., 1977.

Lopez, Barry: *The Rediscovery of North America*, University of Kentucky Press, Lexington, U.S.A., 1990.

Lynch, Michael: *Scotland: A New History*, Pimlico Press, London, U.K., 1992.

MacBean, E.: "The Master Masons to the Crown of Scotland," *Ars Quatuor Coronatorum*, Volume VII, Edinburgh, U.K., 1894.

Mackey, Albert G.: *The Encyclopedia of Freemasonry and its Kindred Sciences*, Moss and Company, Philadelphia, U.S.A., 1875.

Mackie, J. D.: *A History of Scotland*, Penguin Books, Middlesex, U.K., 1964.

McCreath, Peter L. and Leefe, John G.: *A History of Early Nova Scotia*, Four East Publications, Tantallon, Nova Scotia, 1982.

McGee, Harold F.: *The Native Peoples of Atlantic Canada*, McClelland and Stewart, Toronto, Ontario, 1974.

McGrail, Thomas H.: *Sir William Alexander, First Earl of Stirling: A Biographical Study*, Oliver and Boyd, Edinburgh, U.K., 1940.

McQuade, Ruth: "Badge of the Baronets of Nova Scotia," Self-Published, Ottawa, Ontario, 1976.

McQueen, John and Scott, Tom (Eds.): *The Oxford Book of Scottish Verse*, Clarendon Press, Oxford, U.K., 1966.

McPhee, John: *The Spectator* (weekly newspaper) Annapolis Royal, Nova Scotia, March 23, 1993; June 8, 1993; August 31, 1993; May 23, 1995; April 9, 1996.

More, James F.: *The History of Queens County*, Nova Scotia Printing Company, Halifax, Nova Scotia, 1873.

Morison, Samuel E.: *The European Discovery of America*, Oxford Press, New York, U.S.A., 1971.

Nish, George: *The French Regime*, Prentice-Hall, Scarborough, Ontario, 1965.

Patterson, George: "Sir William Alexander: The Scottish Attempt to Colonize Acadia," The Royal Society of Canada, Toronto, Ontario, 1892.

Pohl, Frederick J.: *Prince Henry Sinclair*, Clarkson N. Potter, New York, U.S.A., 1974.

Pohl, Frederick J.: *Atlantic Crossings Before Columbus*, W. W. Norton, New York, U.S.A., 1961.

Public Archives of Nova Scotia: "Royal Letters, Charters and Tracts Relating to the Colonization of New Scotland and the Institution of the Order of Knights Baronets of Nova Scotia, 1521-1638," (F 5221 B37) Halifax, Nova Scotia.

Quennell, Peter: *Shakespeare: A Biography*, World Publishing, Cleveland, U.S.A., 1963.

Quinn, David B.: *North America From Earliest Discovery to First Settlement: The Norse Voyages to 1612*, Harper and Row, New York, U.S.A., 1977.

Quinn, David B.: *England and the Discovery of America, 1481-1620*, Alfred A. Knopf, New York, U.S.A., 1974.

Rawlyk, George A.: *Nova Scotia's Massachusetts: A Study of Massachusetts-Nova Scotia Relations, 1630-1784*, McGill-Queen's Press, Montréal, Québec, 1973.

Reid, John G.: *Acadia, Maine and Scotland: Marginal Colonies in the Seventeenth Century*, University of Toronto Press, Toronto, Ontario, 1981.

Reid, John G.:"The Scots Crown and the Restitution of Port Royal, 1629-1632," *Acadiensis*, 6, Fredericton, New Brunswick, 1977.

Reid, John G.: "Sir William Alexander and North American Colonization: A Reappraisal," Centre of Canadian Studies, University of Edinburgh, Edinburgh, U.K., 1990.

Rogers, Charles (Ed.): *Memorials of the Earl of Stirling and the House of Alexander*, William Patterson, Edinburgh, U.K., 1877.

Ross, James: *A History of Congregational Independancy in Scotland*, James MacLehose, Glasgow, U.K., 1900.

Ross, Sally and Deveau, Alphonse: *The Acadians of Nova Scotia*, Nimbus Publishing, Halifax, Nova Scotia, 1992.

Rowe, Frederick W.: *A History of Newfoundland and Labrador*, McGraw-Hill Ryerson, Toronto, Ontario, 1980.

Sauer, Carl O.: *Seventeenth Century North America*, The Netzahaulcoyotl Society, Berkeley, CA., U.S.A., 1980.

Savary, A. W.: *History of the County of Annapolis*, William Briggs, Toronto, Ontario, 1913.

Scottish Record Office: Guthry, Richard: "A Relation of the Voyage and Plantation of the Scots Colony in New Scotland Under the Conduct of Sir William Alexander Younger," 1629 ("Robert Angus Letter") Nova Scotia Baronets Yule Collection, GD 90, SEC3-23, Templelands, R. H. 11-68, 1, 2, 7.

The Scottish Review, Volume XXXII: "The Knights Templars in Scotland," Edinburgh, U.K., 1898.

Slater, Edmund F. (Ed.): *Sir William Alexander and American Colonization*, Burt Franklin and the Prince Society, Boston, U.S.A., 1873.

Smith John: *The General History of Virginia, New England and the Summer Isles*, I.D. and I. H. for Michael Sparkes, London, U.K., 1624.

Smout, T. C.: *A History of the Scottish People, 1560-1830*, Fontana Press, London, U.K., 1985.

Spence, Lewis: *The History of Atlantis*, Citadel Press, Secaucus, NJ, U.S.A., 1973.

Staunton, Howard (Ed.): *The Complete Illustrated Shakespeare*, George Routledge and Sons, London, U.K., 1858.

Stevenson, David: *The First Freemasons*, Aberdeen University Press, Aberdeen, U.K., 1988.

Stevenson, David: *The Origins of Freemasonry: Scotland's Century, 1590-1710*, Cambridge University Press, Cambridge, U.K., 1988.

Story, Norah: *The Oxford Companion to Canadian History and Literature*, Oxford University Press, Toronto, Ontario, 1967.

Thwaites, Ruben G.: *The Jesuits Relations and Allied Documents: Volume I, Acadia, 1610-1613*, Pageant Book Company, New York, U.S.A., 1959.

Tuck, James A.: "Maritime Provinces Prehistory," National Museum of Canada, Ottawa, Ontario, 1984.

Villiers, Alan: *Men, Ships and the Sea*, National Geographic Society, Washington, DC, U.S.A., 1973.

Wallace Ferguson, Brigitta: "The Scots Fort: A Reassessment of its Location," Department of Canadian Heritage, Parks Canada, Halifax, Nova Scotia, 1994.

Westmore, Donald and Cousins, Leone (Eds.): *The Hugenot Heritage of Some Families in Nova Scotia*, Falcon Press, Kingston, Ontario, 1988.

Whitehead, Ruth Holmes: "Nova Scotia: The Protohistoric Period, 1500-1630," Nova Scotia Museum, Halifax, Nova Scotia, 1993.

Wilmhurst, W. L.: *The Meaning of Masonry*, Gramercy Books, New York, U.S.A., 1995.

Wormald, Jenny: *Court, Kirk and Community: Scotland, 1470-1625*, University of Toronto Press, Toronto, Ontario, 1981.

Yates, Frances A.: *The Occult Philosophy in the Elizabethan World*, Routledge and Kegan Paul, London, U.K., 1979.

Yates, Frances A.: *Renaissance and Reform: The Italian Contribution*, Routledge and Kegan Paul, London, U.K., 1983.

Yates, Frances A.: *The Roscrucian Enlightenment*, Routledge and
  Kegan Paul, London, U.K., 1972.
Yates, Frances A.: *Theatre of the World*, Routledge and Kegan Paul,
  London, U.K., 1969.

AGMV
MARQUIS
Québec, Canada
1997